A Spirit In Motion

Aaron J. Schieding

Phenomena Books

Published by Phenomena Books

Copyright © 2015, Aaron J. Schieding

The right of Aaron J. Schieding to be identified as author of this work has been asserted by him in accordance with sections 77 and 78 of the Copyright, Designs and Patents Act 1988

All rights reserved. No part of this publication may be reproduced, copied in any form or by any means, electronic, mechanical, photocopying, recording or otherwise transmitted without written permission from the publisher. You may quote from this book up to 200 words, properly cited, without permission.

ISBN-13: 978-0-692-51553-2

www.phenomenabooks.org

Cover image © Andrejs Pidjass/Nejron Photo 2015. Used under license from Shutterstock.com.
Author photograph by Josh Johnson

First Edition: October, 2015

1 3 5 7 9 10 8 6 4 2

Contents

Preface		vi
Prologue:	**Tears in the Rain**	1
1:	**Buried in Antiquity**	13
2:	**Stories From Beyond**	27
3:	**In the Hunt**	39
4:	**Forever Faithful**	77
5:	**Darkness, Grey, and Light**	113
6:	**The Art of Death**	135
7:	**The Symphony Within**	147
8:	**A Force Unleashed**	161
9:	**The Scientific Method**	179
10:	**Time Flies When Your Dead**	207
11:	**Ghost in the Machine**	219
Epilogue:	**The Path Ahead**	231
Acknowledgments		243
Bibliography		244
Index		254

Dedication

This book is dedicated to the memory of Nikola Tesla, one of the greatest thinkers, scientists, inventors, and experimenters in human history. He believed in the continuation of the soul after death and was one of the fathers of spirit radios. He dedicated his life to expanding the understanding of the unknown, and to the betterment of mankind.

Preface

AS HUMANS, we all have similar questions, while living our lives on this place called Earth: Why am I here? How long will I have? Is there ultimate truth? While not every question can be easily answered, there are certainly many things that humanity has in common. We all seem to have a spark inside of us that makes each of us unique and different. When people aim for the stars, they can achieve great feats of human will. Every day, one can see acts of courage, understanding, madness, love, and hate. But is the source of these attributes what people refer to as the 'soul'? If so, what exactly is this, and where does it originate? Are humans bestowed a soul from a divine source upon their bodily creation? Or does one just have a simple electric current within themselves, and nothing else?

While not everyone lives to a ripe old age, it can be certain that everybody eventually passes away. No matter how much plastic surgery, antioxidants, or exercise, the end is inevitable. Some people are bothered by the idea that their time is running out, while others don't seem to concern themselves with this fact. One of the biggest questions on the human mind is often whether there is an "afterlife". The famous ancient Greek philosopher Socrates (~469-399 BC) thought that there was something after death. According to fellow philosopher Plato, Socrates once remarked, "The hour of departure has arrived, and we go our ways – I to die, and you to live. Which is better God only knows." He had been sentenced to death, for "corrupting" the minds of the youth of Athens; he also did not go along with the state religion, which did not go over well. Throughout the years there have been others too, who held different ideas about the unknown, and paid the price with their execution.

Today there are many religions, all of which provide their own explanations of the soul and its place in some type of afterlife. Are they all correct in some way, or perhaps only one? Could it be that none of them are right? Here in the land of the living, the complete truth may never be known. What lies beyond, possibly in some other dimension, may really be more than the human mind can comprehend while alive. It is my hope that by reading this book, it will expose your mind to all of the possibilities. It is my sense that humanity is better off when we understand the beliefs of others, so that we can join in a constructive dialogue; one that brings us closer together, moving toward common goals. I hope you enjoy the book, while keeping an open mind.

Aaron J. Schieding

"Whenever you have truth it must be given with love, or the message and the messenger will be rejected."

– Mahatma Ghandi

Prologue:
Tears in the Rain

"The reports of my death are greatly exaggerated."[1]
- MARK TWAIN

AFTER MARCHING for days, we have stopped in-between two ridge-lines, where for the time being my unit seems to be in safety. Like so many other points in our arduous journey, it has become apparent that the appearance of a moment without worry of being run through by a bayonet is, just that, a moment. While one may not always confide in his comrades his fears of death, one look into their eyes is all that's needed to see it. I have been told by Brigadier General Marston that our regiment, the 2nd New Hampshire Volunteers, is currently well over three-hundred men. While I am confident in the willingness of our regiment to bleed for our great Union, it is but a shell of the nearly one-thousand men that left a couple years ago to fight our countryman. Now in the second day of battle in the vast fields here at

---

[1] "And Never the Twain Shall Tweet" (See Bibliography)

A Spirit In Motion

Gettysburg, we have stopped alongside fellow patriots of the 68th Pennsylvania Infantry. Off to our other side are soldiers from our good neighbor back home, Maine. It is our good fortune to be here in battle with such honorable men.

It is now approximately five in the afternoon, our forces in the orchard have sustained numerous casualties and it is uncertain how long we can hold out. I am curious as to what the crows, who have mostly kept their distance, think of all these men attacking the land and filling the air they fly in with filthy smoke. Numerous units have been sent to the southern edge of our position and fired many volleys against the enemy. Many of the treasonous have fallen, though they cannot place the blame on us, they now reap what they sowed. We have been able to suppress the looming threat much of the day with the great Napoleon cannons, and now our commander has told us of the news we feared, that we will soon run out of cannonballs. Our mission as explained is to now move with great speed to the cannons and begin to retrieve them so that they do not fall into the hands of Lee's bootlickers.

July 2nd 1863 - Noon

It is now perhaps an hour after my last entry. I have been shot. I fear my fate may be to never escape this wretched battle. Sarah, I do not know if I will feel your loving embrace again, my wound is hard to bear. My dear wife, please know I have had all intentions of returning to you. I must go now, the men believe that the enemy may charge our position at any minute. I pray that our medics will find me first.
- Lt. Charles A. Hastings

149 years later...

"Mom I hope you enjoyed the tour today, I know I did, I've been dying to visit Gettysburg for years."

Robert's mother Janice took in a deep breath of the grassy air that is characteristic of the former battlefield, scanning the monument-studded landscape. "Well I had a fine time. You know we came here back in 1978, with your father."

Robert grinned. "Well yea, I remember that a little, but I was only five then. I wish I recalled more of it. It's amazing we're here all these years later and I have my own family now, who would have thought?"

"I was so worried when you were a year from college graduation and you were still single," his mother said. "But then you met Jennifer, and now I'm here with my two grandkids. I'm so glad we could come here and spend time as a family, Robert. It means a lot to me."

Janice was now 70 years old and retired, enjoying time to see the world after working so many years. By now night had fallen, and the family had gone back to the bed and breakfast they were staying at for the weekend. Robert wanted to make more than a day-trip out of it, knowing there were so many sights to see and stories to hear.

"Well mom, it's time to head over to that restaurant we passed by earlier. I made reservations for dinner," Robert told her.

"Oh alright son," she answered. "It's been a long day of walking and I'll be glad to sit down to a good meal."

The family left for dinner, coming back later around eight-o'clock.

The family arrived back at the bed and breakfast, and went to head in for the night. "Robert, I think I'll sit on the porch for a little while. It's such a lovely night out."

"Alright mom, I'll be back out to join you in maybe twenty minutes or so."

Robert, his wife, and two kids went inside. At this time, people visiting the battlefields had left for the night, and a calm warm breeze pervaded the starry sky. Janice had heard the stories like others that if you listened close enough you could hear a cannon fire here or a rifle shot there, but she did not hear any. Just then she became aware of a man standing in-front of the porch area looking off into the distance.

He turned to her and said, "Good evening ma'am, what are you doing out here?"

She was a bit startled as she had not noticed him until then. "Oh hello, I'm just enjoying the view on this serene night, and you?"

The man looked befuddled at her response, and seemed to be preoccupied with thought. "No offense ma'am, but this forsaken land could not be less serene. It is nothing but hell on earth in this soldier's opinion."

It was then that Janice became aware that the man was dressed in what appeared to be a union outfit. "Oh you must be with the re-enactors that we had the pleasure of watching this morning near Culp's Hill! You men did a wonderful job, you should be proud of yourselves."

The mysterious man did not seem to be paying much attention to her. "Beggin' your pardon ma'am, but I must go now back to the field of battle. We have been called to defend the orchard at all costs, and not let our cannons fall into the hands of the enemy. You'd best stay indoors."

Before she could respond, Janice was shocked to see the man walk into a nearby open field and vanish! She sat there on the porch rocking chair for a couple minutes dumbfounded, trying to convince herself that it was dark out and she must have not seen him turn somewhere.

"Hi mom, I'm back. Thank goodness there's a TV in the room the kids are staying in, they wouldn't know what to do without one. Mom you look confused, is everything ok?"

She wasn't sure what he would think of what had just occurred. "Well there was a man here, and he had one of those Union outfits like the re-enactors wore when we saw them earlier today."

He seemed surprised. "Oh really? Maybe he lives over this way, or maybe he's staying in a room like we are with other re-enactors. Yea those guys were amazing this morning, it was so realistic."

She looked embarrassed. "Well Robert, ah, I don't think he was one of them. You see he mentioned something about going back into battle in the orchard, I guess he meant the peach orchard. And then... well... he vanished."

"Huh? What do you mean? He left in a hurry, like he ran off?"

"No I mean he walked off into the field here across from this building, and he literally vanished into thin air!"

He laughed saying "Ok mom I think you better get to bed, now you're imagining things. I knew that sun was hot, but I guess we should have stopped to get you some water after the battle re-enactment."

Janice was annoyed by her son's reaction. "You don't believe your own mother? I mean I'm telling you I think he was a ghost!"

Robert grinned. "Right mom, come on, let's go inside it's been a long day. We need to get some sleep cause there's another big adventure tomorrow."

As you probably guessed, Janice was right to be annoyed at her son. The man was not a guest where they were staying, and was not a war re-enactor. As she realized, he was a ghost. The spirit of Lt. Charles A. Hastings! You see, after a medic found him lying against a tree, he helped him up to get to safety. As they were making their escape, a Confederate sharpshooter took aim at Charles, and shot him in the back. He died where he fell, killed by a man he never even saw. Even after the battle was over, and became a tipping point in the war, Lt. Hastings never left Gettysburg. Every day he takes part in the battle that led to his ultimate demise. He has been doing this for 152 years!

Now to be honest, this man never existed; he is a made-up character to illustrate a point. But he is based on numerous encounters over the years that people have had with the ghosts of Civil War soldiers in Gettysburg and other key battle locations. Sometimes people literally talk to the ghosts, or more commonly they just get a glimpse of them. The point is that there is evidence that the afterlife exists. It is not some fantastic notion that some cult of people believe somewhere, or a place that people make up so that they don't have to just disappear into the ground and fade into dust. People often think of their ultimate future as immortality, because it allows us to deal with leaving everything we currently know and love. We know that there is a universe and that the Earth is like a little grain of salt in comparison. But to most people living on Earth, they realize they will never go to space, and this is the planet they know. The events and places in their small life of 75 or even 95 years, is plenty and keeps them busy. As of now, it appears that 125 years is around the upper limit of human life. Even today, with medical labs able to grow a limited number of replacement human organs, there is a question of whether this adds to the quality of life for older patients. Some people don't really think much about death and what happens afterwards, while others probably think about it too much. There is a revelation that you come to after you are done thinking of all the things that make us different as humans, and that is the one thing that we have in common. Death. But what does it mean to die anyways? Do we just become skeletons six feet under when our brain stops functioning and the electricity gets shut off, as atheists believe? Or is there some magical far off place that our souls travel to, to spend the rest of eternity in, as most others believe? These are questions that have haunted–pun intended–humanity for all its history. There are other questions that people ask themselves as well, like "why am I here?" Well, the answer is seven. Okay, not really. This book is not meant to explain everything you've been wondering about existence, but it will help you get to a better understanding of what lies within and about what may lie ahead after your physical time is up.

When somebody passes away, it is like tears shed in the rain. Their chemical makeup is nearly identical, in that they are mainly made up of water. The tears come from the life form, which is made up mostly of water, coincidentally, and are merged with the rain from the atmosphere of the environment they are both contained in. Of course when that person was still alive, they could go outside in the rain, stick their tongue out and let the drops fall onto it. In the end, that rain, one way or another, ends up back in the environment. But when that individual passes on, they have completed the circle of life. Now you may be asking how they have completed the circle if they still exist in another form. The fact is, that the last part of their existence is never-ending as I will explain in more detail later. In that way, the intertwined web of all living things is more like a circle than it is a line. Another way to look at it is that the circle of life is not so much about an individual but about the order of life. The general sequence of life is set a certain way for each life form, and that's just how it is supposed to be.

There are differences in beliefs of the spiritual and afterlife among the many cultures and religions of the world. In the most basic terms though, there are similarities. Most of the world's religions teach that when you die you leave your body as a spirit and transcend the physical plane into another dimension. Many of them say that there is a good realm you can go to and a bad one. Later in this book I will go into great detail to explain to you the similarities as well as the differences between all the major religions. Part of the problem with people not understanding each other is that they do not take the time to discover what people different from themselves believe, and about what really drives them in life. For many people around the world, their religious beliefs form their view of existence. Contrary to how some news organizations make it seem, the majority of the world population get along fine and aren't out in the streets killing one another over their differences. Of course there are always groups of people in some place having some religiously-tied dispute, but that is not necessarily the norm. At the end of the day, humans, on their way to the afterlife, must have common needs. They have to sleep, eat, most have to work, and those who have families need to provide for them, and at times, must rest. After that is all finished and it is time to move on after physical death, it seems that people feel they can believe what they want about the other side without regret in life, because only a select few have died, come back, and lived to tell about it. Those who have had near death experiences have a special viewpoint, based on what they experienced on the other side for the short time they were there. Sometimes what they have seen in the afterlife partially conflicts with their current religious beliefs, and sometimes it doesn't.

Before we really look at what happens after death we must also understand what we are as humans. According to one main perspective, in the Christian Holy Bible it mentions in 1 Thessalonians 5:23 (NIV) that we have a spirit, soul & body. Each one of us is made up of three parts that includes the physical, energy and thought. Most people believe that the spirit and soul are the same thing, but according to this, that is incorrect. It is clear they are different. In Hebrews 4:12 (NIV) it mentions "dividing soul & spirit, joints and marrow..." The spirit is a person's life force, or electricity. The soul is who they are as a person, the feelings as well as the mind's memories. The body is just a temporary shell that the other two exist in, allowing the "entity" to walk physically in the world.

But is this interpretation the 'correct' one? What if one sees the question of the inner being and life after death through a different lens? What of the varying ideas of Buddhists, Christians, Muslims, Jews, Sikhs, Hindus, and others? Why would one group say that a soul could go from a human form to a non-human one, while another religion says that it's impossible? While many people hope that there is an existence after bodily death, they cannot even agree on whether there are positive and negative in those otherworldly realms. Some say that if you did 'evil' things in life, that you must "pay a price" in an afterlife. Others argue that all will be forgiven and one will have eternal happiness.

When thinking of the BC era, one would probably assume that mythology played a large part in people's lives. This is certainly true. Most of the population was sure that when there was a natural catastrophe, it had some divine reasoning behind it. However, there was a group of philosophers who formed what is known as 'Atomism' as early as the 5th century BC. The movement included great Greek thinkers such as Leucippus and his student Democritus (5th c. BC), Nausiphanes (4th c. BC), and Epicurus (4th/3rd c. BC). Their theory basically stated that the Universe and everything in it are made of tiny base particles. There was a similar theory in India around the same time. From the modern viewpoint, they were obviously on to something. They said that there were two principles: atoms and a surrounding void. The atoms, as they saw them, came in different shapes and sizes, and would bounce off of other particles or stick to them. These philosophers came to the conclusion that all of existence is a naturally occurring process. Atomists believed that the 'gods' that others talked about did not really exist. In fact, they believed that there is no divine figure(s), afterlife, or soul. This is quite extraordinary considering the time period. Philosophers who have pondered the very essence of existence, the possibility of an afterlife and other hot topics, generally fall under two groups: pure rationalists and those who want a mix of rational thought with experiences of one's senses. However one's thinking goes, the debates go on to this day.

In 1819, the famed English poet John Keats—who died at only 25 years old—wrote down his interpretation of the soul. He thought that the generally accepted Western concept of the soul being redeemed and going to Heaven through the will of God was too narrow an explanation. Although, he did think that human nature is eternal. Keats explained that we start out as a multitude of divine sparks that are one with God. He calls his overall concept "The vale of Soul-making". He said that we have a spirit which is made up of "three grand materials"; he said these were the intelligence, heart, and the world. According to him, all three make up the soul. However, he also says that one's soul matures over time because of the sufferings of life. He relates this to children learning in a school.

As one can see, there have been many people over the centuries who have not been afraid to find answers to life's mysteries. Even when all but a few believed that gods controlled all things in the Universe, there was still not a complete consensus on who those figures were. With the 20th century came the ability for a great number of people to find out about other's beliefs, even if they were on the opposite side of the world. Today it is not a matter of access to information, but rather an abundance of ideas. The religious teachings remain relatively the same, while there are always new metaphysical ideas to consider. Let us delve deeper now into some of the questions that face all of humanity, starting with a look at the past.

1
Buried in Antiquity

"When the past no longer illuminates the future,
the spirit walks in darkness."[2]

- ALEXIS DE TOCQUEVILLE

THERE IS a land that holds many mysteries, wrapped in a searing heat, where the wind knows no limit. Sand is in overabundance, yet water can be scarce. If one listens carefully enough, the whispers of an ancient people can be heard. In the east is the lifeblood of the country, a wide river, that goes south beyond the horizon. In the most remote of areas, it is as if time stands still. Abundant are the stone inscriptions, which tell of war, the gods, social life, and trade; among many other things. If the people of today strive to fully understand the culture of humanity,

---

[2] Elwell (See Bibliography)

starting from the shadows of the pyramids is a good place to start.

The ancient Egyptians formed one of the greatest civilizations ever to appear on this planet. Many of their great buildings still stand today, and are visited by people from all over the world. Tourists of today are awed by structures and sites like the Pyramids of Giza, the Valley of the Kings, and the Temple of Karnak. For having lasted around 4,000 years, it is a miracle that parts of the ancient Egyptian civilization are still around for us to see today. Although there are modern differences between ourselves and the people back then, there are also similarities. Just as in countries like Britain, of today, there were clear divisions of class in the population. There was the pharaoh, the royal family, government officials, military leaders, the wealthy nobles, priests, architects, influential traders, soldiers, artists, herdsman, fishermen, laborers, and the destitute. Just as most do today, these ancient desert people believed in an afterlife, as well as the soul.

Ancient Egyptians generally had a rough life, and died sooner than those in modern society. It was an accepted fact that one's soul would go on after death, be judged, and be rewarded or sent to the underworld to be annihilated. Most people today are aware of the practice of mummification that went on in Egypt, and can view mummies in museums and on the web. When one dies today, the casket, burial plot, and tombstone are of varying quality and cost; driving by a cemetery, one can see the large monuments versus the small inscribed stones. When it came to death, the Egyptians' place in society also dictated the type of burial, the quality of mummification, or whether they would be mummified at all. Of course, almost all of the famous Egyptian mummies held today in museum collections were considered important figures in their time. The religious belief was that one's soul could return at times to their well-mummified body, and be one with it once more. Mummification was a goal of just about everyone. According to Dr. Salima Ikram, a professor of Egyptology at the American University in Cairo, "poorer people would probably compensate by having prayers and incantations said at the funeral that would speed them to a wonderful afterlife" ("The Afterlife"). As it is today, money talks. Looking at this process from the current day, one might come to the conclusion that wealth won't affect the afterlife. Of course, over a period of thousands of years, ideas about life and death can change quite a bit.

Many religious groups today teach followers that there will be some kind of accounting upon death, a review of the type of life lived, a weighing of positives and negatives. Considering that the majority of current religions came about after the Egyptian civilization, it is not a surprise to find out that they also believed that their lives would be reviewed. As the Boston Museum of Science describes it, when one had died and their body had been prepared, "A priest had to perform the, 'Opening of the Mouth,' ceremony over the mummified body, whereby all the incantations restored all the senses to the body. Speech especially was needed, since the Egyptians had to justify their time on earth upon arrival at the Hall of Judgment" ("The Egyptian"). It was believed that there would be a "weighing of the heart" against that of a feather in the judgment, and whichever way the scale tipped determined one's fate. For this reason, when an individual was undergoing mummification, the heart would be left intact; normally the other major organs would be removed. Before the weighing, the person would have to recall a list of 42 statements, which were called "The Negative Confessions of Maat". According to *Experience Ancient Egypt*, run by Egyptian mythologist and writer Mai Sirry, the dead individual should not have participated in what was included in those statements, which "are like an ancient Egyptian version of the 10 commandments, although they do precede them" (Sirry). Looking through an entire listing of what Egyptians weren't supposed to do, it would beg the question of how any of them could have been deemed worthy. There is a copy of the Book of the Dead, in which these 42 items can be found, on papyrus in the British Museum. In reviewing a translation through University College London, the expectations of the gods were fairly high; this included things such as: one should not take part in evil, say anything bad about the gods, short-change the temple, steal food dropped off at tombs, take milk from kids, stop herds from pasturing, injure others, kill anyone, or make anyone go hungry. ("Book").

After going through various trials of the underworld, and judgment by the god Osiris, if one was deemed pure of heart, it was a smooth trip from there. There have been many findings of artwork in Egypt that very similarly illustrate the above mentioned "Weighing of the Heart". From today's viewpoint, the artwork appears to be a good way of sharing the intended message with many individuals. In an analysis of the trials the dead would go through, the Michael C. Carlos Museum at Georgia's Emory University made the point that "Oddly enough, the Egyptians never seem to have depicted the negative outcome of the weighing, only the joyful individual being received by Osiris and presented with offerings" ("Weighing"). It could be possible that because elaborately carved and painted scenes were often associated with the well-to-do, that showing a less than desirable outcome would not sit well with the elite. Also, people in general probably thought they were decent human beings, and did not deserve to have their souls obliterated.

The majority of ancient Egyptian citizens looked forward to a pleasant afterlife. The paradise realm sewn into the collective religious thought of the nation, was a kind of recreation of the world they knew, yet without any of the downfalls. In a presentation by Dr. John Taylor of The British Museum, detailing the intricacies of the Egyptian afterlife, he describes what all types of people expected. He explains that the goal was reaching "The Field of Reeds", which was an influence for the later Elysium, the Greek's "paradise, the peaceful land where the dead dwell." ("Horizons") It was a realm that was tied to the country landscape which would have been familiar to farmers. Taylor believes that one of the key points of this afterlife was the ability for souls to be at home once again.

It makes sense that "The Field of Reeds" would be enticing for the majority of people; it brought an importance to the quality of burials. If an individual was a poor laborer in the earthly life, the opportunity now came to relive the Egyptian landscape, but with better conditions. This paradise would ensure that a soul could live on forever.[3] This afterlife was said to have been more favorable towards people like the pharaoh and the rich, because their physical bodies had been better preserved. The pharaoh would still be recognized as a god, as they were in earthly life, and had more power than others in the afterlife. From 2006 to 2007 the National Gallery of Australia was host to a traveling exhibition from France, called "Egyptian Antiquities from the Louvre: Journey to the Afterlife". In explaining the history behind the magnificent collection, the art gallery, in relation to afterlife-related artifacts, said that in the Field of Reeds there could be tasks such as "tilling fertile fields, tending fat livestock, hunting in a countryside teeming with birdlife and game, dancing and listening to heavenly music, and fishing in swollen streams" (Campbell). It may seem odd to some people that one would want to hunt or farm in the

---

[3] The realm of Elysium is an example of adaptation of beliefs surrounding the soul and the afterlife through cultures. Later on, the Romans borrowed this realm from the Greeks. In the film *Gladiator* (2000), the hero of Rome, Maximus, goes to the Elysian Fields upon death to be with his family.

afterlife, but apparently Egyptians deemed it normal. Perhaps, happiness really *is* in the eye of the beholder.

The concept of the soul in ancient Egypt was quite different than in current Western religion; it can also be confusing. Other than the physical body, and the heart specifically, there were four major parts to the soul concept: the Ba, Ka, Shut, and Akh. Out of these four, the Ba is the closest connection to what most people in modern times would identify as the soul. It was normally depicted in artwork as a bird with a human head. This aspect of a deceased person could move about between places. In an online exhibition called "Life in Ancient Egypt", the Carnegie Museum of Natural History points out that while there is movement of the Ba between the afterlife and of the living, it was "obliged, however, to return to the tomb during the perilous hours of darkness" ("Life"). The Ka was depicted as two arms raised upward, and was what now would be thought of as the spirit, or life force. Oftentimes the family would bring food and drink to a loved one's crypt after burial, because it was really an offering to the Ka of that body. If the Ba made it successfully through the judgment of Osiris after death, then it could keep its connection to the Ka. In fact, in describing this process, the resource center *Ancient Egypt Online* states that "During the preparations of the body after death, one of the most important things done was the opening of the mouth. This broke the Ba's attachment to the physical body, allowing it to leave" ("Ba"). Of course, as noted earlier, the royals and nobles had much more elaborate tombs, and high-quality mummifications. It was believed that if one's mummy was damaged or not prepared well, the option of having a stand-in statue of the individual was possible, so that the spirit could inhabit that instead. The Akh was often said to be a star in the night sky, and that it was in the presence of the gods. The Shut, pronounced as "shoot", was known as the shadow. This is not the same thing as a shadow on the ground. In discussing the Book of the Dead, the Fitzwilliam Museum at the University of Cambridge England, explains that the ancient Egyptians thought the Shut "to be another part of a person's soul. There are very few pictures of the *shut*; where it does appear, it is represented as a black silhouette with an eye" ("The soul"). According to Ancient History Encyclopedia online, if the burial was not executed in a correct fashion, it was possible that their loved one would become a ghost who would bother the living. (Mark)

Pyramids of the Jungle

In a land vastly different than the deserts of Egypt, there lie the ruins of another great civilization. It is also hot, but with a humidity in the air. There is a great diversity of wildlife, spread across a varied landscape. On a peninsula, miles of beaches are in the north, mixed with lowland, with rainforest in the middle, and highlands in the south. Ancient buildings are found all across the peninsula, covering three modern-day countries. Today, a mix of cultures live on the land, and are visited by tourists each year.

The great Mesoamerican civilization of the Maya came about around 1800 BC, and ended fairly abruptly around 900 AD. The reasons for their general demise are debated to this very day. These 2,700 years represent the main time period for the power of the Maya. Smaller groups survived as separate states, often opposed to each other, until being conquered by the Spanish in the 16th century. The Maya made great contributions to mathematics, including the use of zero. They also were very knowledgeable about astronomy, produced an amazing calendar system based on 365 days, and created the first full writing system in the Americas. The writing consisted of 'logograms' that usually had various parts, which represented whole words, and 'syllabic glyphs' that stood for syllable sounds.

The ancient Mayans believed that they were there because it was the will of the gods, and that they were created by them. This was a polytheistic society, with hundreds of deities. The kings were thought of as gods on Earth, and were the link to the deities. The world was thought of as being flat, as it was in many other cultures of the time. A somewhat familiar theme can be found in Mayan afterlife beliefs, compared to other civilizations; the people believed in a heaven and an underworld. There were a number of key gods for the ancient Mayans; the following are ones that deal with creation, death, and the soul. The one who is thought of as the major creator god was called Itzamna, and is shown in inscriptions, according to The National Gallery of Art (Washington D.C.), as "an old man with distinctive square eyes and a squinty gaze" ("Courtly Art"). There was the god of death, Ah Puch, who was normally displayed as a skeletal figure. He was in charge of the underworld, and was apparently the nemesis of the creator god Itzamna. (Cline) On a side note, for current followers of Western religions, this dichotomy may be reminiscent of the relationship between God and Satan. Another deity that was related to death was Ixtab, the goddess of suicide; oftentimes that form of death, including hanging, was an honorable method. It was said that those who died in this fashion were escorted to heaven by the goddess, skipping the underworld. ("Mayan Gods") She would also bring others to a rewarding afterlife, including "slain warriors, sacrificial victims *[sic]*, priests, and woman who died in childbirth", as pointed out by Encyclopedia Mythica. (Schevicoven)

In the afterlife of the ancient Maya, there are various planes, just as there are in most modern-day religions. There was the underworld, which was referred to as Metnal, or Xibalba; the varying names come from different subcultures. The majority of people would have expected to at least pass through this dark realm. Whether one made it out to paradise would depend on the judgment of deities like Au Puch, based on how good or evil one was. The underworld was made up of nine levels. The realm of paradise was even larger, at thirteen levels; at the top was the ultimate paradise called Tamoanchan. According to the Encyclopedia of Death and Dying, the "heavens" were a "place of plenty, where the souls would be shaded by a tree in the center of the world" ("Maya Religion"). This tree was enormous, with it's roots in the underworld, the trunk going through the human realm, and the top going through paradise. According to Ancient History Encyclopedia, the tree's "limbs can be seen as the Milky Way in a north-south orientation" (Mark, "The Mayan"). This is a simplified view of the Mayan afterlife, as the civilization spanned thousands of years, was made up of different groups, and changed over time.

The Middle Kingdom

It is one of the oldest civilizations, with a rich and varied past. It saw its beginnings largely in the Neolithic period, when the use of tools, creation of pottery and artwork, utilization of farming, and forming of burial practices and spirit worship. As the centuries went by, tribes would form into regional dynasties by the 20th century BC. Just as it was in other regions of the world, kings would come and go, with some respected by the common people, while others were overthrown. Many men would rule with an iron fist, while claiming that they had the 'Mandate of Heaven', which meant that they were divinely approved to rule. The dynastic rulers saw themselves as the sons of Heaven.

By the 5th century BC, China found itself in what is now referred to as the "Warring States" period, in which seven states fought for dominance. Religion and philosophy were an early mix of Confucianism, Taoism, and folk traditions. Confucius (551-479 BC) taught that order was embedded within the Universe, and that Chinese society was an extension of this idea. A king was above society's influential men, who in turn had subordinates, who had wives, followed by children and servants. Confucius went along with the widely-held belief of the 'Mandate of Heaven' because it fit into the need for order among the people. ("The Zhou") By the 4th century, the Nei-yeh ("Inner Cultivation") scriptures were penned, which discussed early concepts of Taoist belief. Professor Russell Kirkland, an expert on Taoism at the Franklin College of Arts and Sciences of the University of Georgia, explains that the text "teaches how to internalize spiritual forces–ch'i ("life-energy"), ching ("vital essence"), and shen ("spiritual consciousness") – through meditative quiescence and purification" ("The Taoist"). The idea was that one should work towards a total stability of self, rather than being torn between reason and moving on emotion. Both men and women could utilize these ideas towards betterment of themselves. Leading up to this time period, as well as during and after, many Chinese also believed that family members who had previously passed on were still around in spirit form. Worship of ancestor's spirits was alive and well.

One king would eventually outpace his rivals for rule over China in the 3rd century BC; the ruler of the state of Qin, Zheng, proved too much for the other dwindling states, and eventually declared himself Qin Shihuangdi. The first man to unite all of China was also its First Emperor. In English, the main body of his name translates as 'August and Divine', which indicates that he would be seen as a deity. He focused on standardization of money, measures, and writing. As the head of the supreme military power in the area, he also used forced labor to build a large wall in the north, which would later become the base for the Great Wall of China. Upon travels to mountains which were considered holy, it is said that he "sacrificed to the gods and communicated with powerful spirits" ("Qin"). Confucianism had been popular around this time, but the emperor believed that Legalism was the best philosophy to use, in order to guide his people. This was the idea that the law must be pushed to keep strict order to people who were, at some level, inherently evil and wayward. Confucian scholars generally believed that citizens would, on their own, see the need for order in the empire and didn't need to be harassed about it. As it turns out, Qin Shihuangdi did not agree, and was also not happy with these scholars analyzing his moves based on what other rulers had done. He banned Confucianism, ordered books burned, and even had many of these scholars put "six-feet-under" while they were still breathing (Violatti).

There was an ironic nature to the emperor's reign; he had no qualms about ordering the deaths of untold numbers of people, but held a fear of dying himself. Not surprisingly, he survived multiple assassination attempts, and did not want to lose his grip on power. In fact, he wanted to live forever, hoping to find a proverbial "fountain of youth". He inquired among his court magicians about how he could cheat death. They told him that they believed there were herbs with extraordinary properties on far-away islands which, if he ingested, would make him immortal. These supposed experts thought that if the emperor sent a large contingent of young people to search for the herbs, they would, being pure at heart, succeed in their mission. Unfortunately for the emperor, after these youths left, they never came back. After traveling to locate the herbs himself, he ended up becoming mortally ill. (Lubow 2) He ordered the construction of his own tomb many years earlier, and planned for family members to be buried there too; the complex was one that would be unrivaled in China. Qin Shihuangdi passed away in 210 BC at the age of 49. He had wanted to enter into the afterlife with company and would, most likely, have appreciated loyal guards or soldiers being interred with him. Over the years, archeologists have found many remains of those involved in the tomb project, nearby in groups. These people were put to death so they wouldn't spill secrets of the tomb's construction. Today, the large tomb site of Emperor Qin Shihuangdi, also referred to as his mausoleum, is famous around the world, since its discovery in the 1970s. Rather than having real warriors entombed beneath the ground, an army of thousands of terracotta soldiers was carefully crafted and setup in formation. As the clay soldiers were given individual looks, they seem to carry an eerie essence to them. The emperor could not escape physical death and his sarcophagus remains closed. However, in a way, this ancient ruler found the eternal life he sought.

2

Stories From Beyond

> "While I thought that I was learning how to live,
> I have been learning how to die."
>
> - LEONARDO DA VINCI

WE HAVE all heard the phrase "and then I saw the light at the end of the tunnel." This could be someone describing his or her drive through an underground tunnel. But in this case we are talking about a different kind of passageway. When most people describe their near death experience, they report that it begins with seeing a dark tunnel and a light at the end. This is one of the connection points between our world and the next. It is generally believed that there are two tunnels, one that goes somewhere nice and one that goes somewhere not so nice.

I had a short brush with death myself when I was a child. I do not recall having any visions or out-of-body experience though. I was in elementary school, and went with my parents to a cookout around a pool. It was a church-related gathering at a church-member's home. I spent some time in the pool floating on some kind of inflated tube. I was not a great swimmer, and spent most of the time near the low to middle of the outdoor pool. At some point I drifted to the deep end of the water, and this is where trouble found me. There was a teenager who was also in the pool, and he started rocking the tube I was on. It flipped over, and I fell in! I swallowed a little water because I don't think I was expecting to fall in as quickly as I did. I remember panicking, as I went further towards the bottom. There were probably at least fifteen other people in the pool at the time, but were unaware of my lacking abilities in the water. I tried my best to swim towards the top of the pool, but I think that because I was a child, the distance seemed far. In reality it was most likely around four feet to the surface. One of the adults became aware that I was in trouble, and pulled me out. I lay on the concrete surface that surrounded the pool, coughing up water. I was in disbelief that something so scary could have happened to me, and that I could have died. Of course with all the people that were there, it was not extremely likely that it would have reached that point, fortunately for me. On the other hand, this same scenario has played out in the news in recent years, sometimes with a fatal end. These types of incidents are certainly a reminder to not take life for granted.

For many centuries, individuals have claimed that when their heart stopped beating for a couple minutes or even hours that they miraculously left their physical bodies and traveled to another place. The stories they have told about what they saw and who they saw stand at the core of our current knowledge concerning the afterlife. The small number of people who get an inside look at the other side help the rest of us uncover the true characteristics of what awaits us all. Most of the NDEs that we hear about are ones where the person visits Heaven. There are also a smaller number of reports from individuals who are given a tour of a place that is the total opposite; a place called Hell. Then there are stories from those who briefly died, who detail seeing the middle dimension, usually along with one of the other destinations in the same experience. There was one in particular I recall reading in which the person sees the middle dimension, where the dead are mixed together with demons and the living. One revelation we can take away from NDEs is that just because people visit a certain place in the afterlife does not necessarily mean that it will be their final destination when they die permanently. Where people go during an experience of temporary death is a reflection of their life up to that point and it shows them what they need to see.

As time goes on there are an increasing number of NDE experiences that detail an OBE (out of body experience) that do not always include the normal trip through the tunnel into the light. A lot of people have a brush with death in the hospital, after an accident, or during a routine surgery. They report hovering over their body near the ceiling or even above the hospital. Many times in these cases they can describe to the doctors and nurses what the staff were doing in detail, even though they the patient were clinically dead for a couple minutes. There are even instances where the patient can tell a nurse what room she came from elsewhere in the hospital, to get to the surgery. Sometimes the person who has experienced the NDE knows what the team was talking about, even though scientifically this person could not know. Interestingly, this type of OBE was described in the Tibetan Book of the Dead, which is said to have originated in the 8th century. In looking at an edited copy of the first English translation, in regards to what will happen at the moment of death, it states, "When the consciousness-principle getteth outside [the body, it sayeth to itself], 'Am I dead, or am I not dead?' It cannot determine. It seeth its relatives and connexions as it had been used to seeing them before. It even heareth the wailings" (*The Tibetan*). In looking at this quote from a Western perspective, it is interesting to note that it seems to line up with many NDEs of today.

Over the centuries, some people who have had NDEs and/or OBEs have declared there to be a 'cord' that connects their 'astral body' to their physical one; more specifically, the cord is said to usually be a silver color and roughly one inch thick. The idea is that these individuals end up moving outside of themselves; descriptions of this shift include floating, being sucked out, or flying upwards. The term *astral* denotes nonphysical existence of a duplicate body that can move through metaphysical realms and encounter paranormal experiences. People who report seeing the silver cord are either hovering over their normal body or are moving away from it. It is said that one can only drift so far, because the cord–which has a stretching ability–will eventually snap! If that happens then the person cannot go back, and their physical body dies. The normally reported attachment points of the cord between the physical and astral bodies are on the head, the navel, the chest, and the back.

The cord is mentioned in the Holy Bible; "Then people go to their eternal home and mourners go about the streets. Remember him – before the silver cord is severed, and the golden bowl is broken; before the pitcher is shattered at the spring, and the wheel broken at the well, and the dust returns to the ground it came from, and the spirit returns to God who gave it." (Ecclesiastes 12:5-7, NIV) The golden bowl, shattered pitcher, and broken wheel, are analogies to the body being emptied of the spirit.

Since NDEs have become popularized over the last thirty years, there has been a push-back from mainstream scientists. Many of them say that the experiences people report are scientifically explainable. Stephen Hawking, arguably the world's most famous physicist, has been clear with his beliefs in this matter for many years. In a 2011 interview with the British newspaper *The Guardian*, he said, "I regard the brain as a computer which will stop working when its components fail. There is no heaven or afterlife for broken down computers; that is a fairy story for people afraid of the dark." (Sample) Hawking represents many like him in the field who say science can fully explain life and death. The common answer from scientists, and many doctors, is that the NDE is related to processes and chemical releases inside the brain upon clinical death. Of course that statement of Hawking's is more applicable to those who die permanently.

The NDE as a concept has been around for thousands of years. In fact, the Greek philosopher Plato wrote about this in his legendary book *The Republic*, which dates to around 380 BC. There was a soldier named Er, who was from Pamphylia, a small region of what was the Roman Empire to the northeast of Israel, and north of Egypt. He was in a battle which led to his death. The bodies of those who died, including his own, laid out in the air for ten days. The bodies started to rot, as they would be expected to, except for his. The army sent his corpse back to his hometown to be disposed of. Two days later, a funeral pyre had been built, and he was lying on top of it, ready to be incinerated by fire.

Er surprisingly woke up on the pyre. He was not dead at all, but perhaps in a coma. He had had a near death experience and wanted to tell everyone about it! He said his soul left his body and moved off with others to a mysterious place. There were two holes in the earth and two leading into the heavens. Each hole represented a one way tunnel. Between heaven and the underworld, there were seated judges. Their job was to look at what that person had done in their life, the good and the bad, and decide their fate. Those who were judged as unjust had some type of symbols attached to their backs that signaled their bad deeds. When it came Er's time to stand before the judges, they told him that he would be sent back to life as a messenger. They told him to remember what he saw there and to report it to people when he got back. The souls who came with him went their separate ways to their fates. Then some souls traveled in to where he was, from both the underworld and heaven, and set up a festival-like camp in a meadow. They seemed like they had traveled a long distance, and some knew each other, even though their fates had been different. The ones who had familiarity spoke and asked each other questions about what it was like in their respective dimensions. Many who came from the underworld wept, for they had been there a thousand years!

In his 1991 book *Asian Folklore Studies*, Dr. James McClenon, a social sciences professor at Elizabeth City State University, included an analysis of NDE folklore between medieval Europe, and China & Japan. The beliefs of these two countries are rooted mainly in Buddhism. McClenon points out that researchers in the West have found some similarities in NDE stories coming from the East. It does not seem unusual that individuals from different areas of the world would hold some of the same basic beliefs, or see similar things in NDEs. Nevertheless, there will always be some differences that are rooted in cultural backgrounds. In discussing important sources of NDE writings from Japan, the author points out that people expected to go to a temporary hell or purgatory, or to the Pure Land. If they went to heaven, they would be brought there or greeted by Amida. He is known as the Amitabha Buddha in Mahayana Buddhism, and the "Buddha of Boundless Light" (O'Brien). If they had bad karma, they would be brought to the lord Yama, ruler of the underworld, to be given punishments.

Stories From Beyond

McClenon talks about a story within a book called the *Nihon ryōiki*. The book, "compiled in the ninth century by the monk Kyōkai, provides the first written Japanese accounts of NDEs"; this "includes the narrative of Kashiwade no omi Hirokuni, who died in 705 but revived after four days" (McClenon). The man saw family members, similar to modern Western accounts, and reclaimed his body due to good karma. This is only one of numerous accounts that can be found in some of the early Japanese texts.

Without question, those who have seen the other side will never forget the experience. The normal major events in life pale in comparison to visiting the afterlife, and returning into the body. In her recent book *Near-Death Experiences: The Rest of the Story*, NDE expert and author P.M.H. Atwater points out, "The majority of near-death experiencers come back as positive 'can-do-ers,' ready to transform themselves, their families, their careers, their religion, their politics, and their pocketbook. Almost immediately worlds collide." (91) These people realize that their understanding of life is now much different. In fact many people who are 'transported' into the world beyond say that when they were communicating with guides or a religious figure there, they either pleaded to stay or be sent back. A lot of NDE experiencers, when met with the brilliant love and peace of Heaven, really felt like they were finally home. In other cases, those who still had young children felt that they would be abandoning them, and asked that they be returned to their earthly lives.

For those who have come away from their NDE with profound revelations, it can make it that much more difficult to re-integrate into society. Some say they were shown truths, like the nature of music, or the existence of many other dimensions, or inventions that could be built to help humanity. There are some experiencers who say that they saw moving holographic imagery that revealed events of the past or the future, or both. Some people are able to bring back this important information, while others forget most of it upon returning to their physical bodies. For those who can recall amazing revelations, they now have a great responsibility of how to deal with it.

One of the earliest NDE accounts featured on television appeared in 1977 in "Life After Death" on the *In Search of...* series, which was hosted by the late Leonard Nimoy. The show covered mysterious topics, and is considered the progenitor of later paranormal and speculative series. A woman, Catherine Hayward, told her story of being diagnosed with Hodgkin's lymphoma, a type of cancer, in 1970. Three years later, at age 27, she found herself in the late stage of cancer. She was in the hospital, lying on a bed, and she watched as the readout on the heart monitor flatlined. She was dead. Catherine says that she left her body and went to the afterlife. Before she left through a tunnel, she saw the medical staff try to save her. Like many others, she saw an extremely bright light at the end of the tunnel. At the other end she met a figure, one who Catherine is sure was God. He briefly spoke to her and told her that there was an unfinished task in her life and that she had to return to her body. She had been struggling with the ravages of cancer and did not want to go back. She was briefly revived, but then went back to the light; upon her second trip to the other side, she said that she was embraced by God. He wanted to know if she was aware of what was going on and she replied that she did. Catherine then fully returned to her earthly body and miraculously recovered. As Nimoy points out, her doctor, three years after her NDE, declared her cancer free. (In Search Of)

In 1999, Dr. Jeffrey Long, co-author of *Evidence of the Afterlife*—as well as other titles—started the Near Death Experience Research Foundation (NDERF) and its website. He also served on the Board of Directors of the International

Association for Near-Death Studies (IANDS). With the help of his wife, Jody, author of the recent release *God's Fingerprints: Impressions of Near Death Experiences*, they have been cataloguing NDE stories from all over the world. She is the organization's webmaster. They see their website's listing of thousands of NDE accounts as a public service to people of all nationalities. For people who want to submit their story, the Longs describe their definition of an NDE as "a lucid experience associated with perceived consciousness apart from the body occurring at the time of actual or threatened imminent death" (Long). They say that their site houses the largest collection of NDE reports in the world. The following are a sampling of three stories submitted to the organization:

A man from France described falling ill with breathing problems, which had to do with water around his heart. He was admitted to an ICU, and was told he needed surgery. He said that he died on the surgery table and found himself in a bright white light. The man felt that he became part of a "universal energy" and could go wherever he wanted without the normal constraints of earthly time. He met his dead grandfather, who conversed with him. One of the unique qualities of his NDE was that he could interact with life at the molecular level and fully understand it. He explained that there was a group of deceased family members, including his grandfather, who revealed his life's objective. They also told him he needed to return to his earthy life. He revealed that by passing into the afterlife, he had access to all knowledge and understanding of the Universe. He also mentioned that he saw no religious figures and, as he did prior to his NDE, does not believe in God. Overall, he is appreciative of his experience and believes it has positively changed him.

A Greek woman told of her experience connected with blood loss while delivering her baby. She grew cold as she felt her life slipping away. While clutching the nurse's cross necklace, she asked if the nurse if she believed in God. The nurse put the cross into her hand, as the new mother left her body. She went to a "pool of light", which she saw as being her true home, where she instantly understood everything. She met multiple members of her family who had passed away years earlier. One of these people was her mother-in-law, who told her that she had spent time with her new baby before it was born. The woman became aware of realities that have been described in other NDEs as well, such as a great library of knowledge, reincarnation, a life purpose for all, telepathic communication, and a vision of the future. She said that this was the best thing that's happened to her.

Lastly, an experience was sent in by a Muslim man from Iran, who had fallen and hit his head. He recounted that the pain was too much and he left his body, and went into a tunnel. He reported seeing imagery of deceased family members in the tunnel. Also, like some other NDE experiencers, he had some kind of a life review. He explained that he saw both good and bad memories. He found out that his whole experience happened, in earthly time, in around 20 seconds; however, this didn't seem possible to him. He found that time on the other side did not exist or did not work the same way as it does here. He told NDERF that he followed his religious beliefs before his experience, and that he still felt they were important after this event. He is still sure that God and an afterlife exist.

The Longs continue to faithfully share the stories of those who want others to know that there is an afterlife. This project is a "labor of love", which hopefully will continue for many years to come. All the people who help them with the website or translation of foreign language submissions are volunteers. The reports that have been dutifully collected provide great data on the NDE phenomenon. As Dr. Long has found, there are many corroborating features of the stories found on his website, such as light beings, tunnels of light, religious figures, relatives, libraries, and much more. The fact that submissions are sent in from many different countries, whose experiencers come from different prior religious backgrounds, helps to back up the validity of the overall findings.

3

In the Hunt

"There is a passion for hunting something,
deeply implanted in the human breast."[4]

- CHARLES DICKENS

IN WONDERING about the great beyond, the search for evidence, for some, may point to ghost hunting. This is not to say that this type of activity will hold all the answers; it will not. In fact, based on my research, if you are on a ghost hunt and communicate with a ghost through a technique like EVP (electronic voice phenomenon), you are only dealing with activity in the 'middle dimension'. That may only be one third of the other side, or probably less, since it *traditionally* just encompasses the Earth's physical plane and possibly just below it. The funny thing is, the

---

[4] Dickens (See Bibliography)

people who are searching for ghosts usually feel like they are hunting them, even though the spirits are present and you just normally can't see them. It's not as if the ghosts are playing hide and go seek; they are sometimes sitting in the chair next to you and to them it's normal. Unlike other deceased people, for one reason or another, many of the departed cross over into the middle dimension. For them the trip wasn't far, and in their own way, they are stuck here just like we are. But just like us, at one point or another, the spirits will move on to their final destination.

It is astonishing to think about how many souls may be in the middle dimension at any given time. You have to figure that all the spirits within the afterlife may account for every human being who has ever existed! Of course nobody knows how many people have been alive, but just based on the current population of the planet, it is some number in the billions! Now I am not saying they are all in one dimension, just that it would be interesting to know what kind of basic percentage of people hang around for a while. One of the most common occurrences of many ghost sightings in one place happen in Gettysburg, Pennsylvania, in the United States. This of course was where one of the largest battles of the Civil War happened. This just gives you a glimpse of spirits hanging around for a long time. Later on I will discuss more about the sequence of time and what it means to the afterlife process.

The development of all the ghost hunting shows flooding TV over the recent years has jumpstarted interest in what happens after death. People will generally gravitate towards certain shows, and not particularly love other ones. I have a couple favorites myself, that I get more out of than others I have watched. My favorite show is *Ghost Adventures* with Zak, Aaron, Billy, Jay, and (formerly) Nick. From a ghost hunting perspective, I find this show contains the most evidence. My other favorite is more of a paranormal inves-

In The Hunt

tigation show called *The Dead Files* with Amy & Steve. This is very different from the other show, but offers a look at the ghost world in an exciting way. In this show, they do not investigate with electronic devices. Instead, Amy claims she can see dead people and talk to them, and Steve is a retired police detective who interviews people involved in a haunted property. The basic concept of these shows is that the people who live or work at a location have had paranormal experiences and want answers about what is going on. For people who do not know much about the paranormal or about how the spirit realm works, it can be a frightening experience. When people buy a home that is old and realize shortly after that it is haunted, it is similar to when humans encroach upon the territory of forest animals. You hear on the news about towns cutting down forest and building out, and having trouble with bears or moose running around the town. Those animals were there first; it has been their home already, and now new creatures are moving in. It is the same way with the dead and the living, because to the dead, the building is still their home.

For thousands of years people have seen ghosts and heard voices just like they do today. The difference is that we now have technology that can be used to interact with those passed on. Sometimes ghosts are not the only thing people see. According to author of paranormal topics, Dr. Leo Ruickbie, objects with direct connections to people, such as ships, can also appear from the great beyond. In fact, on July 11th, 1881, Prince George, then a sailor and the future King George V, wrote in his journal on a ship: that "At 4 a.m. The Flying Dutchman crossed our bows. She emitted a strange phosphorescent light as of a phantom ship aglow" (17). Over the years, many sailors have spotted the ship crossing the sea.

The type of equipment used nowadays on most ghost hunting shows has only been in use by those groups for about a decade. Some of the items such as voice recorders have been around longer. Now we have small infrared video cameras as well as night-vision. There are also small EMF (Electromagnetic Frequency) detectors with lights that turn on when an energy comes close to the device. During relatively recent history, ghost investigators realized that they need to be careful determining what their findings mean when using the EMF detectors. The problem with these is that they are affected by the electric current running through a building. Sometimes they find that there is improper wiring in an older home for example, and that the people living there are experiencing what they think is paranormal activity. What will happen sometimes is if, let's say, one of the family is sleeping in a bedroom that has too many electrical waves being released inside it, they may be having hallucinations. Probably the hottest device starting to be used now is the 'spirit box'. This flips through radio frequencies very quickly so that each one is just a blip and the sound that comes out of the attached speaker is like white noise, but a little choppier. The idea is that the spirits use the radio waves to produce words or sentences that they want to convey in response to questions being asked. The result is that the team hears the white noise and then it is interjected by the voice coming from the other side. This device is controversial and doubters believe that people piece together sounds they hear in the radio frequencies and say it's whatever word they think it is. Or they say that it's actually a word or set of words that made it through the white noise that is coming from a radio station. Other people, like myself, have watched enough instances of the device being used during investigations to believe that we are seeing intelligent responses to questions being asked in a room. I have also used one, which I talk about later on. There will always be those who don't believe, just like there are some people who think Bigfoot exists while others don't. The reality, is that the truth is out there.

It is likely safe to assume that many individuals don't see the reasoning for ghost hunting or communication with the dead. They take the approach that when you pass on, you do, and that's the end of the story. So why bother those who have lived their earthly lives already? It seems the answer to that can be analogous to another question people have asked over the years. Why climb a mountain like Everest? Of course, the answer is because it's there! Human beings have always been curious and have wanted to know the things outside of their knowledge. That is just part of human nature. We want to know what it is that makes us human, and part of that is discovering the transcending time of our lives that moves us into the afterlife.

A lot of times people who become investigators of the paranormal or ghosts have experiences themselves at some point in their life, and they become one of those people who need answers. The great thing is that by going on that quest they can answer questions for themselves, as well as for other people. In the case of a show like *Ghost Adventures*, those answers can be shared with millions of other people. The knowledge that is collected about ghosts and other entities is very valuable in the end to all people. During investigations, it is found that there are different types of entities that reside on the other side. Based on my research, there are seven major types of entities or spirits that exist in the entirety of the afterlife. This is, roughly, coming from a Western perspective. Now each of them will be listed and described, and denoted what dimensions they are in and what type of interaction is possible. The dimensional construct will be discussed many times later on, but the basic premise is that there are three dimensions in the afterlife: Heaven, the middle dimension, and Hell. The concept of there being more than two afterlife dimensions is found in numerous religions.

Doppelgängers

These are perhaps the least known presence that are seen, and are not encountered often. In fact, they do not fit into the list of seven as well because they are not actually in and of themselves entities per-say. They were included because there needed to be an all-encompassing list of what you would discover in other dimensions. However, this is a phenomenon that is known for being seen in *this* dimension. A doppelgänger may essentially be an imprint of a spirit/soul on the fabric of time and space. What is not known at this time is how long these imprints last. Commonly they are of people still alive, and are seen by individuals who know the living source. They have been reported to have been seen when something bad was happening or was going to happen to the real person they are based on. There seem to be many more that go unnoticed, that cannot be seen by the naked eye. From all the known reports over the centuries, it is clear that the body that is spotted is often fully solid. These paranormal incidents are also known as bilocation.

This bilocation phenomenon was actually addressed in the *Catholic Encyclopedia*, the printed books from the early 20th century, which *Catholic Online* describes as "the most comprehensive resource on Catholic teaching, history, and information ever gathered in all of human history". The texts made it clear that the supposed appearance of someone in two different places was rumored to happen, but that it did not really make sense. However, it should be remembered that the Encyclopedia's original publishing occurred over 100 years ago, and that much has changed in the realm of metaphysical research. Mentioned was the assumption that the natural place for the spirit and soul was in the human body, and that it really should not be outside of it without some higher intervention. The explanation goes on to say that certainly if God wills it, this phenomenon could be made to happen, though the true physical body isn't really altered. The text even goes so far as to point out that some noted Catholic theologians such as St. Thomas deny the possibility of the duplicate person, while others like DeLugo think it is a possibility ("Bilocation"). Today, the Catholic Saint Anthony of Padua, a priest from the 13th century, is said to have had the ability to appear in two places at the same time (Richert).

In Norwegian mythology, as well as current day, these Scandinavian people call this phenomenon the "Vardøger". Many times a person would be expecting another individual they know, perhaps a family member, and hear what they thought was that individual coming; then a little while later the actual person would arrive. This experience could be considered a "reverse deja vu" because one seems to be experiencing a real occurrence before it's time. ("Vardøger")

In the local newspaper the *Wirral Globe*, which concerns the population of the north-western Wirral peninsula in England, a story of doubles was recounted. Over forty years earlier in England, two nineteen year old women, along with one of their teenage male cousins, decided to take a day-trip. They took a train to a nearby town. One of the women, named Terri, hoped to run into a man she knew years earlier from school, named Paul. At an art gallery, an old man spoke to her, asking her why she wasn't with Paul, yet she didn't recognize this gentlemen. A bit later a young man asked Terri how her mother was, because he heard she wasn't doing well. In fact, her mother was fine. Like the first man, she did not have his acquaintance. However, he knew her last name! Later, a woman was surprised to see her, because she said she thought she was in another town. In another strange occurrence of the trip, a young man asked Terri if she was marrying Paul. Before leaving the train station, Terri saw herself and Paul in the window of another train! Years later Paul had been working abroad, and then moved to Australia. Terri's friend Ruth was visiting there and ran into the man. In talking, she told him what happened in England, and he insisted that at the time he was in fact engaged to her friend! (Slemen)

A TV episode of the paranormal investigation show *The Dead Files* revealed what seems to be another aspect of the doppelgänger phenomenon. In the episode, the physical medium Amy was in the business they went to go see that had been having trouble with paranormal activity. As it turns out, there had been a murder there fairly recently. This was mostly what was causing the employees to be spooked, even though they did not know that at the time. Amy also reported that there was an entity which sounded like it was a demon that was in the basement as well. She was able to see the murderer inside the business and what he looked like. Well, the amazing part about it was that her investigative partner Steve looked into the murder and found out that the man convicted was still alive and in jail within driving distance! Part of how she conducts her visit is to have a professional sketch artist draw the people she sees at the location, and the picture matched the convict! So the murderer left a doppelgänger at the location unintentionally. The question would seem to be, will it vanish when he actually dies in prison? Or will it stay there forever? It is currently unknown what type of communication, if any, is possible with doppelgängers.

Finally, in regards to a well-known historical person experiencing the doppelgänger of themselves, there is the story of 18th century German poet Johann Wolfgang von Goethe. In his autobiography, he said that once when he was riding his horse in-between towns, he observed a man riding towards him, not an uncommon occurrence back then. However, when the rider was to pass him, he saw that it was his older self wearing a different outfit! Almost a decade later, he was again on the same dirt road, but riding now in the opposite direction. He came to realize that he was wearing the clothing that his younger self had seen on his older self years earlier! According to Sascha Karberg, journalist and Knight Science Journalism alumni fellow at MIT, some medical professionals believe experiencers of the phenomenon could be having visions because of brain tumors or epilepsy. (Karberg)

Ghosts

When people think of spirits coming through in one way or another from the afterlife, they usually think of ghosts. For thousands of years people have caught glimpses of ghosts fading in and out of our physical space. Usually they just walk through a room and then vanish. Rarely do they ever make an effort to communicate to the living witness. As you have probably surmised already, ghosts are spirits of the dead. They are people who've passed on and reside for a time in the middle dimension. Although, some would say they are just a figment of our imagination, including the ones caught on film. Sometimes when somebody is in a haunted location they actually see a ghost appear, and it is dressed in clothes of the period they come from. That is how it should be, since everyone comes from a distinct point in time.

In ghost investigations, the spirits will literally appear on photographs or video recordings. Sometimes they will appear as a whole figure, or part of one. Many times this will be categorized as ectoplasm. That is when a ghost is trying to materialize by utilizing energy which is shared between the two dimensions. It is not always clear whether the ghost is always trying to get the attention of the living people in the room or if they sometimes do this when no one is around as well. There are different theories about why a ghost would sometimes appear somewhat solidly and interact with the living. Personally, it seems to me that, perhaps, they are sometimes people that never intended on dying and wish they could come back and hang around a location. It is like someone who tried to buy tickets at the door to a popular concert and was shut out because they ran out of seats and is yelling to be let in.

It has been discovered over the years that there are two categories of ghosts. There are interactive ones and non-interactive ones. Based on other evidence such as audio recordings or multiple sightings of the same ghost by different people, it seems that some are just replaying an event in their life and aren't paying attention to the living. There is a story that was told by a well-known comedian/actor recently about a series of strange paranormal occurrences years ago at an apartment of his. He lived in a building about five stories tall, and he would see a man running through his apartment away from other men. The ghosts were dressed in clothes from the mob era around the 1930s. He saw them numerous times, and they would disappear through the wall. He eventually found out that the building later on had had a couple floors added onto the top, and that his floor used to be the actual roof! He also discovered that the building was a hot-spot for gangsters from the Italian mob. It turns out that there were some reports that in some instances, if somebody didn't pay up on a debt they owed to the mob, they would bring them up to the roof and throw them off! He was basically seeing the event leading to the ghost's death, but in that case they were non-interactive ghosts. It is unknown if these ghost types literally see the living and ignore them, or if they don't actually see us at all because they are blinded by their own reality. As far as interactive ghosts go, they are able to communicate in a number of ways. As mentioned above, they will oftentimes appear so the living see them. Their presence is felt sometimes by investigators when the living get goosebumps or their arm or neck hair stands up on its own. This is due to the use of electricity by the ghost. The spirits can also lower the temperature in part of the room so that the living can feel it. This is because of the exchange of energy to the ghost from the heat. Ghosts are energy, so it makes perfect sense that they can absorb other energy. At other times, ghosts will move objects in a room to get the people's attention. This is similar to turning on electrical devices like TVs that were previously off. Lastly, the other major tool they use to communicate is through audio recording devices, so that the living and the dead can speak to one another. Ghosts as described can only be found in the middle dimension, and as stated some of them can have two-way communication with the living.

The soul that is moved through death is sometimes greatly fractured, and in some cases very dark. Not all ghosts are the same, because not all people are the same. There are some who call ghosts 'lost' spirits rather than 'heavenly' spirits. It is safe to say that for some people, the concept of the lost spirit is a controversial one, and they do not want to believe that they may become one, or that a loved one has passed on to this place. Of course, many people who seemed for the most part to be average human beings to friends and coworkers may have ended up as lost spirits. As a note to ghost hunters, if you are spoken to by a spirit and are not sure if it is evil or not a ghost at all, you can test it with questions. There are some paranormal investigative teams that do this, and they sometimes ask logical questions. For Catholic or Protestant investigators, Christianity offers their followers a tip in 1 John 4:1-3 (NIV), where it states,

A Spirit In Motion

"Dear friends, do not believe every spirit, but test the spirits to see whether they are from God... Every spirit that acknowledges that Jesus Christ has come in the flesh is from God, but every spirit that does not acknowledge Jesus is not from God." Believe it or not, there are actually some Christian teams that do investigations.

In the epic Greek poem *The Odyssey*, written by Homer around 2,800 years ago, lost spirits are described. The main character Ulysses travels in his ship to the end of the ocean, which back then was considered the very edge of the world. In the BC era of course, people generally thought the earth was flat. Ulysses reached his destination, which it turns out was the entrance to Hades: "When lo! Appear'd along the dusky coasts, Thin, airy shoals of visionary ghosts: Fair, pensive youths, and soft enamour'd maids; And wither'd elders, pale and wrinkled shades; Ghastly with wounds the forms of warriors slain..." (Homer). Essentially he is saying that he spots all types of people, young to old.

When seeking confirmation of ghosts, one can look at truths laid out by those at the very core of religious belief. In Luke 24:36-39 of the Holy Bible, after the resurrection when the apostles are discussing hearing of Jesus' return, it reads, "While they were still talking about this, Jesus himself stood among them and said to them, 'Peace be with you.' They were startled and frightened, thinking they saw a ghost. He said to them, 'Why are you troubled, and why do doubts rise in your minds? Look at my hands and my feet. It is I myself! Touch me and see; a ghost does not have flesh and bones, as you see I have.'" So there you have it. Jesus apparently makes it clear that ghosts exist! One thing we can be sure of is that the global population will probably see more and more ghosts every year, because more people die every year! However, adherents of some Eastern religions may technically disagree.

In The Hunt

The position of Islam on the subject of ghosts is different than some other faiths. The majority of adherents believe that "ghostly" sightings are not human spirits at all, but instead are what are known as 'jinn'. This is a 'race' of spirit beings that Allah was said to have created from fire, who live parallel to humans, and were created before people existed. It is written in the Noble Qur'an (Sahih International translation, 23:99-100): "[For such is the state of the disbelievers], until, when death comes to one of them, he says, 'My Lord, send me back that I might do righteousness in that which I left behind.' No! It is only a word he is saying; and behind them is a barrier until the Day they are resurrected." This could be seen as reasoning for the lack of human ghosts.

An example of a person who many in the general population would probably say went to Heaven would be Mother Teresa, Ghandi, or the prophet Abraham. Some people believe that spirits such as these can visit the middle dimension temporarily, but that their home is in Heaven. Normally within this framework, they would not be called ghosts, if they were in the heavenly dimension. Whether direct communication is possible would most likely depend on the theory of temporary visits to the middle dimension. Otherwise direct talk would not be possible. Although to throw another wrench into the situation, many people also believe that within a short period of time after someone dies, they can visit their family one last time before crossing over through the tunnel of light. The concept of non-linear time would possibly allow for that, in the face of possible objections.

It should be noted that in the Holy Bible, there is an apparent case of a visitation to the Earth by someone who died many years earlier. In Mark 9:2-8, Jesus leads three of his disciples, Peter, James, and John up a high mountain. When they reach their destination, the deceased prophets Moses and Elijah materialize next to Jesus as he transfigured (meaning that he assumed a more divine appearance, the same as he would appear in Heaven). It says "his clothes became dazzling white, whiter than anyone in the world could bleach them." The prophets were speaking with Jesus, although it does not mention what about. Now, it should be noted that most Christians and Jews believe, based on scripture, that Elijah was one of only a handful of people ever to be taken in history to Heaven while alive. On the other hand, Moses clearly died, yet he appears standing there on the mountain! When they are done talking with Jesus, a cloud envelopes all of them and they hear the voice of God himself, and the cloud leaves and takes the two prophets with it. Either Moses was literally there as a spirit or it was like a projected image of him in Heaven, however the latter seems unlikely. Then again, it clearly means this is an extremely unique case and that obviously Moses was one of the most revered people to ever live, and is an important figure of many major religions in the world. Thus, if you have a grandfather and he went to Heaven, you will probably not run into him on your hike up a mountain.

Shadow People

This is a class of entity that people have only started really looking into fairly recently in the media, but have seen for many centuries. They have most likely been around just as long as regular ghosts have, but based on paranormal investigations it now seems that shadow people are somewhat different. The obvious reason for the name given to them is that they do not appear as ghostly apparitions or as an energy orb, but as a shadow figure. Usually they are literally pitch-black, like they are absorbing light, which they may in fact be doing! Many people also describe the figures as having reddish eyes, which are just points of light. There have been cases of people shining a flashlight into a shadow person and the light being lost in it, which in a way resembles a black hole found in space. It is believed by some that they are all negative entities, but this has not been proven conclusively.

Not surprisingly, the majority of scientists do not think this is a true paranormal phenomenon. Explanations include hallucinations in the time of falling asleep or waking up, or not having good vision out of the corner of one's eye (Anissimov). Of course it is the nature of those in the science community to be skeptical of the unexplained, unless it can be proven in an experiment. Other people say that depending on the building, window locations, and lights outside, that shadows can be cast into a structure. This certainly is the case sometimes, but not all. In a study detailed in the science journal *Nature*, researchers in Switzerland and the U.S. discovered a possible connection between the brain and the sense of a shadow person. They found that while assessing an epileptic patient before surgery, if there was "focal electrical stimulation of the left temporoparietal junction" of the brain, the patient might describe something like a shadow person (Blanke). However, it would seem that due to the nature of this study, only a minority of experiencers would be affected by these findings.

In the "Shadowman" episode of the paranormal investigation show *Ghost Lab*, which aired on the Discovery Channel, the team found a mysterious moving shadow at an antiques mall. A video camera was set up in a room in a store, when there was nobody in there after-hours. After an alarmed door opened on its own and the alarm sounded, team members checked it and found no explanation. The footage from a video camera nearby was checked, and there was a shadow moving across the floor. One of the team members went to the room to walk by the spot where the anomaly occurred, so he could recreate a shadow moving across the same spot. His shadow could be seen, but the others watching the camera feed noted that when he walked by, it created a vibration of the camera, as well as of a chandelier in the room. In the original footage of the mystery shadow, there were no vibrations detected. One of the team leaders also discovered that a temperature detector near the shadow occurrence registered an increase of around ten degrees, and then went down ten when the shadow left. The mystery was not able to be definitively solved; whatever caused the shadow to move in and out of the video frame was beyond the camera's view ("Ghost Lab").

Many people who have reported encountering shadow people, whether one or multiple times, tend to note the swiftness of these dark figures. Although, there are the reported exceptions, where a person says they were watched while in bed. Over the last few decades there have been some in the world of paranormal study, such as prolific author Rosemary Ellen Guiley, who've worked to crack the enigma of shadow people. Guiley, the author of over fifty titles, was interviewed recently by *Psychology Today* magazine, which has been around since 1967. She said that after much research, she came to the conclusion that not only are shadow people real, but they are the earlier mentioned djinn (jinn) of the Islamic beliefs. Of course, this is just her personal opinion. She pointed out that the djinn have not really been part of the conversation in the West, because it has remained mostly within the Middle East. Probably the strangest aspect of the shadow person phenomenon have been the corroborating accounts of many of the figures wearing a long coat and rimmed hat. Guiley thinks the shadowy figures often do this to hide a not-quite-right human shape. She said this had to do with stories from long ago that stated the djinn could "not duplicate 100 percent of a human body" (Ramsland). Whether the author is on the right track or not, in the eyes of those interested, remains to be seen.

Animal Spirits

This is one subject that often sparks debate when talk of the afterlife comes up. Many people ask the question of whether their family pet travels to the afterlife when they pass away or if they just cease to exist entirely. The response depends on what part of the world you live in for the most part, or on what your religion is. At least that covers the theoretical part. This also brings to the front the fact that humans are the most intelligent species on the planet. The correlation with that, belief-wise for many people, is that humans have a spirit and an attached soul and animals have a more basic spirit & soul. This would mean that if some poachers kill two members of an elephant family in Africa, those elephants feel the pain of dying; not only that, but according to the non-human soul concept, the poachers will be placing the burden of the killings on the souls of the surviving elephant family members. There are many vegans as well who see animals as having souls, and for this and other reasons believe it is not right to kill and eat them. On the other hand, most societies encourage eating animals as part of their diet, and the Christian religion has historically been supportive of animals being used as a food source, except on occasional 'sacred' days.

The belief that animals and plants have some form of soul is called Animism. When it comes to groups of people holding this belief, the majority of them are found in Asia. In turn, you can find some form of the belief mainly in Buddhism, Hinduism, and Shintoism. The major religion in Japan is Shintoism, and the belief in non-human souls is illustrated in numerous anime movies produced there. Oftentimes these movies show, for instance, animals of the forest as souls after they have died and present the angle that this is part of the never-ending circle of life. It enforces the idea that even though the animal died from old age or was hunted, it lives on as energy.

In the Holy Bible, in Ecclesiastes 3:19-21, the Israeli king ponders:

> Surely the fate of human beings is like that of the animals; the same fate awaits them both: As one dies, so dies the other. All have the same breath; humans have no advantage over animals. Everything is meaningless. All go to the same place; all come from dust, and to dust all return. Who knows if the human spirit rises upward and if the spirit of the animal goes down into the earth?

Later in the Bible, in Revelation 19:11 (NIV), the Apostle John in his vision from God, concerning the Apocalypse, says, "I saw heaven standing open and there before me was a white horse, whose rider is called Faithful and True." Here we have someone seeing an animal coming out of heaven, which is of course part of the afterlife. Following this in verse fourteen it actually states that the armies of heaven follow, and they are all riding on white horses. Based on religious beliefs and people's near death accounts, it would seem that non-human souls would be found in the middle dimension, and that risen spirits are reunited with their pet's souls in heaven. It would seem to make sense as well that communication beyond the normal is not possible with living people, unless of course you are one of the those people who say that your dog talks to you. In that case you probably need to seek medical help immediately.

In The Hunt

The proper Catholic answer to the question of a soul within other creatures does not really leave much room for speculation. What if the life-form is more basic, like a plant? An answer to this riddle was put forward by *Catholic Answers*, a longtime web resource whose motto is "To Explain & Defend the Faith". Their staff says that animals and plants both have souls. Surprise! However, it is made clear that these souls are just basic material ones, inherent to living things. They differentiate a material type, for plants & animals, and a "spiritual soul" which only humans have. The answer points out that we have a high intelligence, and that we can love others. Unfortunately for owners of "man's-best-friend", Catholic Answers believes that when your dog's time is over, they are truly gone ("Do animals").

Many people are curious about whether their pets will live on after death, regardless of their background. Humans feel a special bond with their pet companions. What does the Jewish faith say about this? To find out, let's see what Rabbi Nechemia Coopersmith says. He answers questions on *Aish*, which is the largest Jewish content website. The Rabbi reveals that he has a dog, and thinks the world of her. He even says he has thought more highly of his dog than of some humans he has met over the years. According to him, the souls of people versus animals are not level with each other. He points out that we integrate morality within our lives, and that this is not something one finds in animals. Also, people can pray or celebrate a heavenly master, while animals cannot. The Rabbi also explains that the Torah, the Jewish holy book, says an animal's basic soul is found in its blood. Even though he says that humans have a higher form of soul, that doesn't mean anyone should look down on animals. As the Catholic answer also says, he concludes that pets do not make it to the afterlife (Coopersmith).

The Sikh religion, which was born in India, adheres to the belief in reincarnation; the majority faith in India, Hinduism, also follows this train of thought. The idea is that not only will people's souls be reborn as different humans, but that it's possible for rebirth to happen in an animal form. Sikhism sees the soul, in any form, as being an eternal one. They believe that an individual can only tell right from wrong while in human form. This means that if one is living as an animal, it will be impossible to get out of the series of revolving births ("Sikhism"). This latter concept seems somewhat similar to the "higher versus lower" soul theme, which was found in Catholicism and Judaism.

In the most well-known ancient Indian text, the Mahabharata, an account is told of a king called Yudhisthira. He and his four brothers fought in a large war and won. Later on, the five brothers went on a final journey to the Himalayan Mountains. In the process of moving higher up to the pinnacles, all four of Yudhisthira's brothers careened down to their deaths. His brothers were heavy with sin, but he was not. The surviving brother was able to make it to the top of the world; he was closer to the gods than any other human. Brahma, the Creator, knew he was coming and wanted the king to come up to the heavens. Brahma had Indra, the supreme head of the demigods, go to fetch him in a flying chariot.

Now Yudhisthira had been joined by a mysterious dog. This canine was following him wherever he went. The king appreciated the loyal aspect of this new companion. He was told his brothers had made it to Heaven but that he would ride the chariot there in his physical body. He wanted the dog to go with him. Indra told the king, "There is no place in Heaven for persons with dogs. Besides, the (deities called) Krodhavasas take away all the merits of such persons. Reflecting on this, act, O king Yudhishthira the just. Do thou abandon this dog. There is no cruelty in this." The king replied by saying he would not give up one who was so devoted to him, until he himself had passed away. Indra replied by pointing out that, "Whatever gifts, or sacrifices spread out, or libations poured on the sacred fire, are seen by a dog, are taken away by the Krodhavasas. Do thou, therefore, abandon this dog. By abandoning this dog thou wilt attain to the region of the deities." Even with this and further reasoning by Indra, the king would not go without the dog.

According to the story's narrator, Vaishampayana, the dog then changed form into the god Dharma, who symbolized righteousness. It was revealed earlier in the story that Dharma is really Yudhisthira's father. He was elated that the king had shown great compassion towards him, supposedly a mere dog. The transformed being told the king, "On the present occasion, thinking the dog to be devoted to thee, thou hast renounced the very car of the celestials instead of renouncing him. Hence. O king, there is no one in Heaven that is equal to thee" (*The Mahabharata*). If the dog had actually been what it seemed, it could have been in the incarnation of a person. However, since the dog would be a lower life form, it would not have gone to the realm of the gods. This is not to say that a dog would somehow be inherently negative in some way. If, in the dog's next life, it were to take a human form, then it could go to the heavens upon bodily death.

Demons

There are not a lot of sources to explain the introduction of demons into the middle dimension. There is one text that comes from the oldest section of the Book of Enoch, dating to the BC era. This book is one of the ancient texts which was excluded from most of the Christian and Jewish holy books. It can currently be found in use by the Jewish group Beta Israel ("Beta"), the Eritrean Orthodox Church, and the

A Spirit In Motion

Ethiopian Orthodox Church ("Book of Enoch"). Coincidentally, the Ethiopian church claims that it's guarding the Ark of the Covenant in Ethiopia. It should be noted that this book is strictly rejected by most religious groups, and whether it is completely accurate as history is questionable. Although for some scholars and students of religion, 1 Enoch is more widely accepted than the second and third books. In 1 Enoch 1:8-12 it states:

> And now, the giants, who are produced from the spirits and flesh, shall be called evil spirits upon the earth, and on the earth shall be their dwelling. Evil spirits have proceeded from their bodies; because they are born from men and from the holy Watchers is their beginning and primal origin; they shall be evil spirits on earth, and evil spirits shall they be called. [As for the spirits of heaven, in heaven shall be their dwelling, but as for the spirits of the earth which were born upon the earth, on the earth shall be their dwelling.] And the spirits of the giants afflict, oppress, destroy, attack, do battle, and work destruction on the earth, and cause trouble: they take no food, but nevertheless hunger and thirst, and cause offences.

These are the children, the Nephilim, of the fallen angels who are described in the next section. In the book of Enoch they are called the Watchers. It mentions in 1 Enoch that there were two-hundred Watchers. This is also referenced in Genesis 6:1, a book accepted by all Christian and Jewish groups. It reads, "When men began to increase in number on the earth and daughters were born to them, the sons of God saw that the daughters of men were beautiful, and they married any of them they chose. Then the Lord said, 'My Spirit will not contend with man forever, for he is mortal; his days will be a hundred and twenty years.' The Nephilim were on the earth in those days—and also afterward—when the sons of God went to the daughters of men and had children by them. They were the heroes of old, men of renown." So essentially, the fallen angels mated with human women, and their immediate offspring were hybrids. As a side note, for fans of shows like *Ancient Aliens*, the Nephilim explain some of the advanced knowledge that early humans had and why a lot of the knowledge was lost until thousands of years later. It would be great to delve into this theory, but that could literally take an entire book to devote to. It is also mentioned that a general life-span was set in motion that had not existed prior, and that people can live up to one-hundred twenty years old. This still holds true today, and is interesting when you consider that before modern medicine, many people did not live past their sixties.

The basic explanation then for the birth of demons was the death of angel/human hybrids called Nephilim who became destined to roam the middle dimension across the earth wreaking division among humans. Unlike regular people, their bodies when born were not matched with created spirits from the realm of Heaven. The fallen angels were never meant to go and mate with human women, so their offspring were not meant to be. What this means is upon their offspring's death they could not enter into Heaven and became the first demons. Just like people in history who have been cast out of societies because they were too different and were not accepted, these original demons were rejects. The last time they were recorded being mentioned was in the book of Numbers 13:33. Moses sent tribal leaders from the Israelites to explore the land of Canaan, and when they came back most of them claimed they could not take over the land. They gave a "bad" or "evil" report saying they found cities that were home to giant men who were the descendants of the Nephilim. Most scholars seem to think the report was "bad" because it was false, not that it was embellished. But either way, the point is that people of the post-flood era had been taught by their parents about the existence of the race of giants before the flood. The Nephilim have been the only beings in history, other than the fallen angels, supposedly to have been eternally barred with no possibility of entering Heaven. Demons themselves are very well documented throughout the world, and are sometimes discovered in paranormal investigations. They are located in the middle dimension. In Homer's *The Odyssey* the ghost of a man called Elpenor tells Ulysses he curses the demons, and calls them dire ministers of woe. During paranormal investigations, two-way contact with people has been documented.

The well-known concept of being possessed happens when demons enter into a human at the spirit level. There are many documented cases throughout history of possessions, as well as fictional accounts such as the movie *The Exorcist*. One story dates back to the time of Jesus and is related in the Holy Bible in Mark 5:1-13 (NIV), which reads:

> They went across the lake to the region of the Gerasenes. When Jesus got out of the boat, a man with an evil spirit came from the tombs to meet him. This man lived in the tombs, and no one could bind him any more, not even with a chain. For he had often been chained hand and foot, but he tore the chains apart and broke the irons on his feet. No one was strong enough to subdue him. Night and day among the tombs and in the hills he would cry out and cut himself with stones. When he saw Jesus from a distance, he ran and fell on his knees

> in front of him. He shouted at the top of his voice, "What do you want with me, Jesus, Son of the Most High God? Swear to God that you won't torture me!" For Jesus had said to him, "Come out of this man, you evil spirit!" Then Jesus asked him, "What is your name?" "My name is Legion," he replied, "for we are many." And he begged Jesus again and again not to send them out of the area. A large herd of pigs was feeding on the nearby hillside. The demons begged Jesus, "Send us among the pigs; allow us to go into them." He gave them permission, and the evil spirits came out and went into the pigs. The herd, about two thousand in number, rushed down the steep bank into the lake and were drowned.

One key difference can be seen right away: the fact that because of who Jesus was, he was able to command the demons by voice alone and they left, whereas exorcists today face a more difficult and prolonged battle. We can also draw from this account the fact that more than one demon can inhabit a human body. An explanation of what occurs after an exorcism comes from Luke the Evangelist in the Bible. He was one of the 70 disciples after the original twelve apostles.

In Luke 11:24-26 (NIV), he says that "When an impure spirit comes out of a person, it goes through arid places seeking rest and does not find it. Then it says, 'I will return to the house I left.' When it arrives, it finds the house swept clean and put in order. Then it goes and takes seven other spirits more wicked than itself, and they go in and live there. And the final condition of that person is worse than the first."

One thing ghost hunters need to understand is that if they capture EVPs, they sometimes need to dig deeper to figure out who is actually talking. Many Christians warn others that they could really be talking to demons because they can fake being a person. During an investigation by the *Ghost Adventures* crew, they had split up and two of them caught a recording on one floor. When they listened to it, it was clearly the third guy yelling something to them. The only problem? That guy was on a different floor and he never yelled to them! So he listened to the recording and said it sounded just like him, that basically the voice pattern was his, but it was *not* actually him! They came to the conclusion that it was a demon impersonating him!

Angels

In Hebrews 13:2 of the Old Testament of the Christian Bible, or known as the Torah to Jews, it mentions that we should be hospitable to strangers because you might just be in the presence of an angel. This means it is not a human being, just an angel disguised as a person. In regards to this tip, it is talking about good angels. There are also different types of angels with different areas of responsibility. One of the major categories is that of archangels. They are like the commanders in an army who report to the four-star general. Most world religions have specific views on the topic. In the Roman Catholic Church there are three recognized archangels. There is Gabriel (Daniel 8:15-17), Michael (Jude 1:9), and Raphael (Tobit 12:15). The latter angel is not officially recognized by Protestants because that particular book is not included in their version of the Bible.

Protestants are split as to whether Gabriel is an archangel. In the Eastern Orthodox Church, they recognize the three mentioned, as well as Uriel (III Esdras 3:1, 5:20), Sealtiel (III Esdras 5:16), Jegudiel, and Barachiel. Some Eastern Orthodox members accept an eighth angel called Jerahmeel. Also, the Ethiopian Orthodox Church includes another angel called Saraqael (1 Enoch 20:7). In Islam, the list of archangels includes Gabriel, Michael, Israfel, Azrael, Ridwan, Maalik, Munkar & Nakir, and Raqeeb & Atheed ("Archangel"). In the Bible, there is an account of a vision to Daniel while he was next to the Ulai canal, who at the time was about to be appointed as the third highest ruler in the kingdom of Babylon by King Belshazzar. In Daniel 8:15-17 (NIV), he says, "While I, Daniel, was watching the vision and trying to understand it, there before me stood one who looked like a man. And I heard a man's voice from the Ulai calling, 'Gabriel, tell this man the meaning of the vision.' As he came near the place where I was standing, I was terrified and fell prostrate. 'Son of man,' he said to me, 'understand that the vision concerns the time of the end.'" So here he actually sees two angels, and one of them is the well-known Gabriel.

Many people accept the existence of guardian angels. There are some people who've reported meeting their guardian angels during an NDE, and that it communicated with them that it has been with them since the beginning of their existence. Muslims believe they have two guardian angels for each of them. People see both male and female angels. In fact in Zechariah 5:9 in the Holy Bible, the prophet of the same name says, "Then I looked up – and there before me were two women, with the wind in their wings! They had wings like those of a stork".

There are also fallen angels who, in the beginning of time, resided in Heaven. At that time they were not bad, but good angels. The leader of the fallen angels is Satan, but as an angel he was called Lucifer. The Christian, Jewish, and Muslim religions all believe he was created by God and resided in heaven, but that he became rebellious and was kicked out. In the Qur'an (7:11-18), there is a description of the intended relationship between humans and angels. It is explained that Allah wanted the angels to bow to Adam, which all except Iblees (Satan) did. He told Allah that he was superior to Adam (and humanity) and would not bow. Allah told Iblees that he was a disgrace and was banished from Heaven. Iblees is not destroyed, but waits for the end of the world. In the meantime, he will work to corrupt humanity, so people will sin against Allah.

Lucifer was powerful, but in the end he and his cohorts were no match for their creator God. In the book of Revelation, John is shown a vision of the future and he sees that Satan will stage a final war against Heaven to get back at God and his angels. He led a rebellion against God, and his followers fought against the arch-angel Michael and his supporters, as is related in this quote from the Holy Bible: "Now war arose in heaven, Michael and his angels fighting against the dragon. And the dragon and his angels fought back, but he was defeated, and there was no longer any place for them in heaven. And the great dragon was thrown down, that ancient serpent, who is called the devil and Satan, the deceiver of the whole world-he was thrown down to the earth, and his angels were thrown down with him" (Revelation 12:7-9, ESV).

Since they were thrown out of heaven, they ended up locked away in the abyss of Hell, which is documented in 2 Peter 2:4: "...God did not spare angels when they sinned, but sent them to hell, putting them into gloomy dungeons to be held for judgment." There is also another reference to the event in Isaiah 14:12-15 (NIV), which states, "How you have fallen from Heaven, O morning star, son of the dawn! You have been cast down to the earth, you who once laid low the nations! You said in your heart, 'I will ascend to heaven; I will raise my throne above the stars of God; I will sit enthroned on the mount of assembly, on the utmost heights of the sacred mountain. I will ascend above the tops of the clouds; I will make myself like the Most High.' But you are brought down to the grave, to the depths of the pit." The Holy Bible identifies a lead fallen angel, a kind of right-hand prince of Lucifer's, called Abaddon. It says in the book of Revelation that at Armageddon an angel causes the shaft in the earth, which leads to the Abyss, to open and that streaming out of it would be locust-like creatures that would cause havoc on the people. "They had as king over them the angel of the Abyss, whose name in Hebrew is Abaddon, and in Greek, Apollyon" (Revelation 9:11, NIV). As has been established, because of the early split between angels, there are now bad and good ones. Including both categories, they can be found both in Heaven and in Hell. Current knowledge would seem to indicate that two-way communication only happens sometimes with good angels who are observing on earth disguised as humans. So, essentially good angels can occasionally be found in the world of the living, which makes them unique. Also what people refer to as guardian angels would technically be in the middle dimension, making angels the only category of entity that can be found in the living realm and all dimensions of the afterlife.

God

There are many names used along history and cultures to describe the supreme-being, the creator. Names used by Christians include Yahweh, Abba & Jehovah. The Jews call him Elohim or Adonai. Followers of Islam use the term Allah. Other Muslims who are not of Arab origin sometimes use the Persian name Khoda. For Native Americans, there is the term Gitche Manitou, or the Great Spirit. The commonality between the religions is that God is all powerful and is the one who created the universe. In Colossians 1:16

(ESV), it states, "For by him all things were created, in heaven and on earth, visible and invisible, whether thrones or dominions or rulers or authorities—all things were created through him and for him." Another understanding of all the mentioned religions is that God is all-knowing, all-powerful, and everywhere at once. Unlike the other entities that you could find in the afterlife, you would not see God in the same sense that you could the others. God is not our size, unlike a ghost, who you could just walk up to. It seems that the reality is that before and in the afterlife you would sense the presence of God rather than meet him face to face. Many religions do not exactly see it this way, however. The Christian perspective is the one being used here, as they teach that those who reach the gates of Heaven are met by Jesus, and that he is the human representation of God. This determination of who you might deal with if you reach Heaven is not going to be accepted by many, but as with religion in general you cannot always come to a consensus.

For those who are atheists, or want to focus on a purely scientific explanation of the universe, they do not see a need for the divine. This means that things don't "happen for a reason", and that one is not necessarily 'destined' to be someone great. However, the 9th century thinker Al-Kindi, considered the father of Islamic philosophy, formed a cosmological argument partly based on earlier Greek philosophy. Many Western ideas were considered and expanded on farther east. In fact, Al-Kindi is quoted as saying, "We ought not to be embarrassed of appreciating the truth and of obtaining it wherever it comes from, even if it comes from races distant and nations different from us. Nothing should be dearer to the seeker of truth than the truth itself, and there is no deterioration of the truth, nor belittling either of one who speaks it or conveys it" ("Al-Kindi"). He said every living thing that appears in the world had causation, just as the world itself did. He believed that God must have made these things happen. The concept of the Cosmos appearing out of nowhere did not seem to make sense. Later on in the 11th century, the Persian theologian Al-Ghazali analyzed Al-Kindi and others' work and came up with both agreements and criticisms. He agreed that God was the cause for all things. Although, he said it was only possible for God to be eternal, and that everything else must have started at some point in time. In years to come, many other great thinkers have pondered these same questions, including the Christian theologian St. Thomas Aquinas.

In a rebuttal to these ideas, Thomas Ash, creator of *Atheist Ground* online, wrote an article entitled "The Case Against The Cosmological Argument" (Ash). In it he admits that the argument is probably the best avenue for trying to prove the existence of God because explaining how the Universe came into being is mind-boggling. He refers to the fact that people often bring up questions surrounding the concept of the 'Big Bang'. As an aside, I recall prodding my college astronomy professor about this, and he admitted that scientists don't exactly know how the 'Big Bang' could have occurred. Ash indicates that although some would say there is a starting point set-off by God, there isn't really any reason why our universe doesn't go back infinitely. He says that people just have a hard time wrapping their heads around the concept that time could really just be a fabrication. Ash also points out that Aquinas claims God is infinite, after saying that nothing has this characteristic. Obviously the Catholic theologian believed God was not bound by the natural laws that he would have set. But Ash thinks this is just a way of getting around an inconsistency. Either way, at the end of the article, the author says that he and those he criticizes really don't know how the Universe started; he still says that the Cosmological Argument doesn't prove that God exists.

A Spirit In Motion

A small slice of the population falls in-between—or aside of, according to some—the theists and atheists, and they are called agnostics. Those identifying as such leave the door open to the possibility that God or gods exist. At the same time, they don't claim to have the answers to questions of the divine or the source of the Universe. This also applies to the concept of souls. Agnostics sometimes see pure atheists in a similar light as unyielding theists.

Of course, for Eastern religions there are often many gods involved in their faiths. Oftentimes, there is a hierarchy of the divine. In Buddhism, there is not a definite god that is the Creator and that has absolute control. Hindus say the creator god is Brahman. In the West, any lesser gods are often referred to as demigods; those types of figures also showed up in ancient Greek mythology.

Followers of the largest organized Jewish movement, Chabad, believe that souls inhabit just about everything, including animals and plants. They draw a direct connection between the Creator and the human soul. Without this link there would be no reason for people to have a soul. They claim that this divine aspect is what makes humans special, with a spiritual need to join with the Creator. Members of Chabad are taught that as each soul is assigned to a physical body, that the Creator gives it a mission to accomplish while in that vessel (Tauber).

Those are the seven main entity types of the afterlife. They inhabit that which we cannot see, and are our counterparts in our shared existence.

When it comes to many paranormal investigations, the knowledge that can be learned is amazing. The reason you need a professionally-minded team to go into a place is because the owners usually are clueless when it comes to the spirit world. Sometimes they are just dealing with a simple haunting, but other times the depth of what is going on in a structure is quite large. Some of the best paranormal research groups have a diverse set of members. It is good in some cases to get a member who is a slight skeptic, who can keep more of an open mind. It is also beneficial to have a scientifically-minded person who can analyze evidence in a methodical way to make sure a natural explanation is not there. In a lot of teams you have an individual who is a die-hard-believer in ghosts and is enthusiastic in the search for evidence of the afterlife. Many teams have a tech person who knows all about the devices that can be used to investigate, such as an infrared-camera or motion sensors. Some groups also include a physical medium who can see and talk with the dead. Probably the key thing for ghost hunters to keep in mind is they need to have a love for what they are doing. The best thing to do is to go into an investigation really wanting to uncover the truth, and to be able to provide evidence in the end that will prove activity to property-owners or people watching on video.

An Investigation Unfolds

Reviewing episodes of ghost hunts from some of the most recognized paranormal groups can be quite a learning experience. One can see what type of equipment is used, various group dynamics, methods, and types of activity occurring. The investigation shows one often sees on television are either accepted by viewers or not. There are those who go into it already believing in an afterlife, who see spirits as making sense. Of course, the ones who are "on the fence" about the whole thing are usually willing to keep an open mind. Then there are people, like many atheists, who don't believe in spirits, an afterlife, or deities. There are exceptions within the atheist community, however, who think our conscious energy survives in the Universe due to metaphysics. When I was just starting to piece together the basis of this book, I decided that to get a true understanding of ghost hunting, I would need first-hand experience.

By October of 2012, I had decided to form an investigation team with two others, Anthony and Tanya, so that we could scout a good location to check out. I wanted to explore mysteries for myself, instead of just trusting others. Doing some research online, we found the Old Meeting House in Sandown, NH. It is the oldest meeting house in the state which is still maintained, and can be utilized for various gatherings. The structure was built in 1773, and has a designation on the National Register of Historic Places. The building was a very active place for town members over the years, and was also used for voting purposes; this includes the 1789 election of the first American President, George Washington. The building is very spacious, with room for a couple hundred people, and has very high ceilings. It has two floors, with balcony seating, and also has a pulpit that stands in-between the separate floors. With a donation to a local society that takes care of the building, the team was able to secure a night for a paranormal investigation.

The team brought a collection of tools to utilize during the investigation. We had two infrared video cameras for capturing anything our eyes couldn't see. We didn't have to use regular lighting, as this was a night investigation. We would navigate in the dark by looking at the camera's LCD screens, or from any moonlight seeping in through the windows. Each camera was attached alongside a separate IR light, on a handheld mount. A handheld digital thermometer with light-up screen was also featured to detect any changes in temperature. It is thought that ghosts cool the temperature around them because they are utilizing heat

In The Hunt

energy as a source of power for manifestation. A major tool that was used was the P-SB7 Spirit Box, made by ITC Research, which enables live communication with spirits. It is a handheld device with a pull-out antennae that operates by rotating through AM or FM radio frequencies in a matter of milliseconds. The user can use the device's built-in speaker to hear the frequency rotations, which sound like blips. Our team, as most professional ones do, chose to hook the spirit box up to a separate speaker that can fit in one's hand. The concept is that a spirit will use the radio frequencies to carry their voice, which occurs over numerous radio frequencies (stations). The fastest scan rate available will speed through five to ten frequencies in one second. The team also had an EMF (electro-magnetic field) detector, which detects changes in electro-magnetic frequencies around the device. There was also a digital recorder, so we could record any EVPs (electronic voice phenomenon), which would be voices appearing that did not belong to any of the team members. Additionally, there was a digital still camera, flashlight, and a laser pen (for pointing things out in the dark).

Our team spent at least a couple hours inside the location, and used our detection equipment in all areas of the building. We performed our first EVP recording session in one of the rear pew boxes in the balcony seating. After a series of questions, and then playback of the voice recorder, there was one instance of a male responding with "no". After this we sat in the middle of the ground floor and started a spirit box session. When I asked how many people were in the building, a man responded with "four", and then a woman said "eight". Right after this there was a woman who said, "Sorry Tim". What was interesting about this was that she did not come through on the spirit box; she was recorded directly onto the voice recorder. Then when I told the team that I heard the response listing the number of people at eight, that same woman spoke again, confirming my understanding with a "yup". The man whom the female spirit was referring to, Tim, must have been someone she was speaking with on the other side. Earlier in the investigation, Anthony was joking a bit during a recording session. Now on the ground floor, he asked, "Are you angry with me about joking around with you earlier?" As soon as he got to the word "angry", a male spirit came through and said "yea". Then about ten seconds later, a female voice was recorded saying "thank you". These voices were coming through on the FM frequencies. We then switched to AM, and asked again how many people were in the building. Ghost hunters will sometimes ask this question more than once because the spirits would be energy only, and could move in and out at high speed. This time we received four responses in a row from all different individuals, and they all put the number of people at ten. It is unknown whether the answers included the three team members. It was asked if "they" wanted to tell us their names, and a man answered with what sounded like "Jeff". Later on, I was with Anthony upstairs, and we were standing at the edge of the balcony overlooking the bottom floor. He had tripped a couple times because of the darkness, and I was worried he could fall from the first row over the balcony. He was heading down that row, and I told him we needed to be careful and that he might want to try the second row instead. As I was saying that, a female spirit was recorded on the voice recorder, saying "you're okay" in an old American or European accent. Soon after, Tanya and Anthony were talking about a particular spot on the ground floor where they thought had a strange feeling about it. As Anthony and I were getting ready to go back downstairs to meet up with Tanya, another EVP appeared on our voice recorder. The voice was male, apparently referring to the spot which was being discussed; he said "already told ya you shouldn't go right there". His voice was so clear on the recording, it was a bit shocking. At the end of the investigation, we caught an apparent energy sprite on infrared camera, shooting quickly up towards the ceiling. By energy sprite we mean it was a defined light anomaly which appeared on camera out of nowhere, could be seen for half a second, and then vanished into thin air. The last evidence we picked up was on one of our IR video cameras. Tanya mentioned that she thought the spirits liked to "talk over her", and a male EVP was recorded in response, which said "no".

Based on all the paranormal evidence the team collected, it would be safe to say that the investigation, from a technical point of view, was a success. We were able to prove that capturing EVPs can be done fairly easily, and can be analyzed on a computer through looking at audio wave forms and spectrum. Critics of the spirit box technology say that investigators are hearing radio station interference and piecing together bits of audio in their heads that sound like words that fit the questions asked. However, though this can occasionally occur, when a recorded voice stretches over five to twenty frequencies, the explanation of skeptics can be ruled out. The world of paranormal investigation is certainly not for everyone, and is frowned upon by some for religious reasons. Our team did not do any investigations past this one; for myself, I had already believed in the afterlife and the soul beforehand, and the outcome of the findings did not change anything for me personally.

4

Forever Faithful

"Faith is taking the first step even when you don't see the whole staircase."[5]

- MARTIN LUTHER KING, JR.

AS IT GOES with many things in life, religion also plays a role in death. It guides groups of people across the planet in their views of the afterlife. How many different views there are within a country depends on how many religions are within its borders. In some nations, more than ninety percent of its citizens are of one particular religious group. In other countries there is a huge variation in beliefs, which is something you would find in many democracies. To really understand why religion holds some of the key answers concerning the afterlife, we need to look at all the major religions of the world. The following

---

[5] "Rev." (See Bibliography)

will detail the six largest religions. There are hundreds of organized religions, but there is not enough room in this book to cover them all. Each faith below includes an exclusive interview with an expert on that religion.

Buddhism

The largest percentage of practitioners per country is in Cambodia at 96.9% ("Cambodia"), followed by Thailand at 93% ("Thailand"), and coming in third is Burma at 90% (Fuller). An interesting fact about Buddhism that many people don't realize is that it originated in India. This is largely a non-theistic religion.

Although Buddhism is a global religion, which is becoming popular in the West, I looked to its birthplace of Southeast Asia to find an expert guide. I contacted Kechara, a Tibetan Buddhist organization, located just outside Kuala Lumpur, Malaysia. I was particularly drawn towards them after happening upon the story of their founder and spiritual leader, His Eminence Tsem Tulku Rinpoche. He is from Taiwan, was adopted by a Mongolian-American couple, and grew up in New Jersey. He ended up running away to Los Angeles at 16 years old and met his "root guru" H.H. Zong Rinpoche, who would go to India and wanted his disciple to follow. Three years later, he had saved enough money–though his guru unfortunately passed away in that time–and he went to India in 1987. There, in northern India, he was ordained as a Tibetan monk by His Holiness the 14th Dalai Lama, who belongs to the Gelugpa sect of Tibetan Buddhism. In the 1990s, he was asked to travel to Malaysia by one of his gurus to raise money for building living quarters for monks from Tibet in India. Later, in 2000, he started Kechara.

Forever Faithful

Kechara has various operations in Malaysia, serving locals and devotees visiting from other countries; they have Kechara House, which is their main center of Dharma teaching, as well as a soup kitchen, helping to feed the urban poor. They are also working on opening the Kechara World Peace Centre, "the future spiritual sanctuary and alternative learning center in Malaysia." Kechara is part of the Gelugpa sect of Tibetan Buddhism. Under the leadership of H.E. Tsem Rinpoche, he took the unorthodox approach of ordaining pastors in the organization so that they can help him spread the teachings of the Buddha. I was honored to be offered the services of Senior Pastor Han Nee Lim, to shed light on the beliefs of Tibetan Buddhism.

Han Nee Lim, a mother of two, is a retired secondary school principal. She retired in December 2000 after a 30-year career in education. She obtained her Master's Degree in Education at Leicester University in the UK at the end of 2001. Over the coming years, she sought answers to questions she had on her spiritual path. In 2004, many of her questions were answered upon attending a retreat taught by H.E. Gelek Rinpoche.[6] Then she was introduced to Kechara and H.E. Tsem Rinpoche by her sister. This is when she found her calling, studying the Dharma and her guru's teachings. In 2012, Lim became a full-time pastor at Kechara House and now works to help others through Dharma teaching.

Unlike most Western religions, Buddhists believe in reincarnation. They see all people as being on a hopeful path toward Enlightenment; this is the escape from the "wheel" of rebirths, when there is full awakening to understanding of life, pure knowledge, and wisdom. It is the achieving of

---

[6] A Tibetan Buddhist monk who gives talks globally, and is the founder of Jewel Heart International in America. His great-uncle was the previous Dalai Lama, and Gelek was part of the monastery group that fled Tibet during the 1959 invasion by the Chinese. Tibet/China relations are still tense to this day.

"buddhahood", following the path set by Shakyamuni Buddha. When one reaches this point, they become empty of all want and there is no limit to the ways they can help other beings. Lim points out that there are "opportune conditions" to achieving human life. This means that, although one might not realize it, being reborn into a normal human form is not common or easy. She explains, "Chances of gaining this rebirth again are as rare as a blind turtle (who swims up to the ocean's surface only once every 100 years), trying to get into a yoke that is floating around constantly on the surface of the ocean" (Lim). She says that one should not focus just on this life they are in and on the things one acquires; death forces us to leave our belongings behind, and move on to the next rebirth. The true focus should be on reaching Enlightenment.

Lim believes, as many do, that we live in a time of moral decline and disorder; this leads to distractions on the spiritual path. She explains that these diversions cause "strong delusions and mental afflictions of people, such as desires, lust, hatred, jealousy and anger. People chase after money and relationships and success and fame, that flounder on the sands of impermanence and change, in a never ending cycle of pursuits. People are caught up in the eight worldly concerns of comfort and discomfort, profit and loss, fame and notoriety, praise and blame." Unfortunately, these human conditions are widespread and clearly evident in today's society. Lim is in the perfect position to appreciate the positive reinforcement of a guru, who helps to guide the way to Enlightenment. However, she says that even for those with a Spiritual Guide, it is hard for people to let go of the "I". We are used to having things our way, and seeing our lives in a way that comforts us. Over the years, a person settles on their version of how life should be. When one's guru presses for change within that student, they push back. According to Lim, "We refuse to turn inward and reflect in what is within us, as the Guru points out, that needs to be removed." Yet, one must be willing to accept the need to become less focused on one's self. If a person does not actively fight against what Lim calls "negative delusions", then he or she wanders off the path to enlightenment.

When it comes to the use of modern technology by Buddhist followers, and whether it is helpful or not in their spiritual lives, Lim concludes that it can be both. There is obviously a prevalence nowadays of computers, smartphones, and other internet-connected devices. But she says that how we use these technologies in the larger picture is important. Lim explains, "If we employ them for the benefit of others, if we use them to promote Dharma (Buddha's teachings), and to enhance our teaching of Dharma, to bring benefit and greater happiness to all, then they will be no hindrance in the spiritual life of Buddhists." Kechara, for example, utilizes web videos to allow people to watch events at their facilities they may have missed, and to deliver teachings by H.E. Tsem Rinpoche. In this way, a Buddhist organization like theirs can reach a global audience. Kechara also holds web chats with those who have Dharma questions, which are answered by either His Eminence or his pastoral team. Also, many Buddhist monks around the world who've embraced the power of social media are able to give inspirational messages to their followers; gurus, such as Kechara's own Tibetan Lama Tsem Rinpoche, can get to the heart of personal issues that their followers have. Lim wants people to consider how they can help others through technology, and not for greed or simply their own material needs.

In Buddhism, as in other Eastern religions, there is the belief in "Samsara", which is the previously-mentioned reincarnation and all of one's actions throughout their many lives. In Tibetan this is called "khor ba", which is "the continuous flow". Every human accrues karma, which can be good and bad, affecting each incarnation. One can either move up to a higher realm in their next life, or a lower one. If one has moved in the wrong direction in their human life, then they may be reborn into the Animal, Ghost, or Hell realms. One can also go the other direction with good karma and possibly go to the Demi-god or God realms. However, if one does not eventually reach the perfect state of Nirvana, then his or her good karma can be exhausted and this person will be reborn into a lower realm. Lim says that if one's karma is bad enough, he or she will go to the Hell realm, and cannot move on until all of their bad karma is exhausted. She exclaims, "It is a place of tremendous physical suffering. There are hot hells and there are cold hells. With the hot hells, there are different types of hells – the Hell without Respite, the Hell of Continual Resurrection, the Hot Hell, the Extremely Hot Hell, and so on." If one is to work towards Enlightenment, the best chance one has is to be born in the Human realm. The key is to follow the Buddha's teachings, while being as pure as possible and assisting others in need. Also, one cannot reach Nirvana by hoping to stay in one of the upper realms of Samsara, because they will become content and forget about studying the Dharma.

An important concept within reincarnation is "anatta". This means that through rebirths, one's self is never permanently fixed to any one realm. In describing this more fully, Lim says, "If we are born a spirit, as our karma dictates, we will also bear the aggregates of form, feeling, perception (or discrimination), compositional factors and consciousness. If we are born in a formless realm, we will not have the aggregate of form. On the basis of our aggregates we impute 'labels'. Examples of labels are a child, a college student, a parent). Our forms are impermanent. When we die, our five aggregates disintegrate and we will assume a new form with a new rebirth (only the subtle consciousness goes from lifetime to lifetime)." All of this lends itself to an intriguing question, one that is woven into this book; what is going on when people see ghosts appearing out of thin air? I asked Pastor Lim if this is in conflict with anatta; she says it is not. It is connected with the Spirit realm, which is technically the "Realm of the Hungry Ghosts". Lim explains, "Beings are reborn there as a result of grasping and not being able to let go of the people and things of this life, not being able to let go of Samsara. It is greed and miserliness that sends people to this realm in rebirth." For those who worship their mansions, sports cars, and huge bank accounts, they could easily end up in this realm. For others, never getting over the loss of a soul-mate could bring them there. In that rebirth, individuals must work through these problems in order to escape the ghost state.

For Buddhists, there are many realms of existence and possible rebirths of the self. Thus, for adherents, the realization of paranormal happenings is not out of the question. However, Lim points out, "Many people are not willing to recognize the fact that there are beings around us and that there are paranormal phenomena occurring all the time". She relates this thinking with those who can't accept their eventual death. Yet, many people do have an interest in these phenomenon, including her own Guru, and Lim explains, "This interest, translated into action–the conceptualization Paranormal films–is directed towards creating awareness that *these beings are real*." The problem, as she describes it, is that the majority of people's karma and level of "attainments" is not conducive to seeing dimensional beings. Of course, for some people today, they won't accept anything that they can't physically see with their own two eyes. According to Lim, it is good for people to gain an awareness of these other beings; this is important because it will "lead us to *develop compassion for them*, as they are suffering too". She says these rarely seen entities, along with ourselves, are all on the wheel of samsara. Lim continues, "Beings in the Spirits realm or Hungry Ghosts realm, face perpetual hunger and thirst. They do not have the karma to see food as food or water as water. All they see is pus and blood." She also says that people who are aware of beings–who are normally invisible to the "living"–should understand that we are all connected together; this is due to previous lives, and the chance that a ghost could have been related to you in a past incarnation. Finally, Lim says it is fortunate that the Buddha provided the Dharma, which tells people that they must consider their bodily death. She says one must meditate on this, because what state one is in at death dictates his or her next rebirth.

Hinduism

In India, around 80% of the population is Hindu. With around 1 billion adherents, this is the third largest religion in the world. There is also a large Hindu demographic in Nepal and–percentage-wise–Mauritius. This is both a polytheistic and monotheistic religion.

For my introduction to Hindu spiritual beliefs, I traveled to Boston, a familiar city for me. I had the honor to meet Swami Tyagananda, a Hindu monk, who is the head of the Ramakrishna Vedanta Society. He has been the spiritual leader there since 2002. After living in India for over 40 years, he was assigned to the Boston location in 1998. The society has had a permanent presence in the city for 105 years and has been at its current location since 1941. Vedanta is one of the major schools of Hinduism and is based on the ancient Vedic texts. Before coming to America, Swami graduated from the University of Bombay and then served in four monasteries from the 70s to the 90s. He is also

Forever Faithful

the Hindu chaplain at MIT and Harvard, as well as having authored and edited numerous papers and books.

In Hinduism, death is not the end; it is another beginning. It is believed that the soul survives the death of one's body and, in most cases, goes through a process of rebirth; this is called reincarnation. Before this can occur, however, those who knew the deceased must deal with the death in their own familiar way. In Western countries, most people will end up being buried in a cemetery, preceded by a wake and funeral service. Family and friends sometimes meet for dinner after the burial to discuss their memories of the loved one. On the other hand, Hindus prefer cremation of the body. As Swami pointed out to me, there are Christians and Muslims in India, so burial is practiced there. In fact, after Indonesia, India is home to the second largest population of Muslims. It is not unheard of to see cemeteries there, as one would in America. Due to the beliefs of those in Abrahamic religions, Swami says that in these religions "There is this idea of preserving the body. Hindus don't feel the need to preserve the body. It is only a shell" (Tyagananda). He gives an analogy of a homeowner who moves away. If someone sells their home and moves to the next one, and the first home is later demolished, it does not really matter what happens to the first house. In India, the 'house' of the soul is dealt with soon after death. Swami explains, "There is a bathing of the body, and chanting of prayers before the body can be burned." Cremation happens soon after and ceremonies and rituals can continue for up to thirteen days later. There are prayers from family for the departed for a good journey into the various planes of existence.

The fact that Hindus believe in reincarnation allows them to see their earthly lives, as well as the 'other side', in a different way than those who reckon on having only one life to live. If one has made many mistakes in life, or has been born with a disfigurement or illness, then there is the hope for improvement in the next incarnation. I asked Swami, "For those Hindus in India who have faced lives of hardship and poverty, do you believe that reincarnation is reassuring for them?" He responded, "Yes, but on the other hand, it is good to keep in mind that it is not simply poverty that brings unhappiness and pain." People who are affluent can also face these things. Some poor people, who he has seen in India, are content. He has also seen people who are wealthy, but are miserable. This is also a common occurrence in America, where gossip magazines love to publish stories about the troubles of rich celebrities. The process of reincarnation rectifies the results of one's karma, which is determined by the decisions and actions of a person in their earthly life.

Hindus believe that karma is a natural process that applies equally to all souls. Of course, this does not mean that people are seen as equal in all human society. In Western religions, it is sin which guides a person to a particular afterlife result. I queried Swami, "Do you think the Western religious concept of spiritual sin is comparable with karma?" He doesn't think it is. He explains that in the Judeo-Christian theology, sin is an act of disobedience to God and/or his commandments; in Hinduism this is not the case. He poses the question, "How do we explain people who are born in very challenging situations, and those born in very affluent situations?" He tells me, "Karma theory helps answer those questions." Hinduism does not bring God into it like the other religions. Thus, these questions must be dealt with differently in other belief systems. Swami explains that because it is not God that is doling out punishments or rewards, "We are responsible." It is up to people to make the right decisions and act with good towards others in life. Yet, there is also a difference in what

Hindus believe is waiting for them in the hereafter, compared with religions like Islam. Swami points out, "Both Heaven and Hell are finite in Hinduism. They are not eternal." For Hindus, the soul keeps moving through the realities of existence and does not get stuck forever in good or bad planes. For example, in Christianity, a murderer could face eternal damnation in Hell. However, in Hinduism, karma will determine the next appropriate rebirth of that individual's soul.

One of the topics I cover in this book is near-death experiences and what these may mean. I asked Swami about noted differences and similarities between NDE accounts of people of different faiths. According to him, when people have NDEs, they have preconceived ideas about what should be in the afterlife. He raises the question, "Is what we see outside there because it *is* there, or because I believe in it?" Many neuroscientists doubt that anything spiritual or otherworldly is going on during NDEs. Where they are coming from is a material world. Religion is trying to say that "the spirit is independent of what is going on in the brain." These are different world views. "Yes, there is something deeper. All people have access to higher realities." When people express what they have experienced in NDEs, the words will be different. Hindus believe that all the religions of the world are true, and they all have the same experiences, but one's interpretation of the experience "will depend on one's own background." Swami explains that Hindus believe you have to experience truth for yourself.

Just as followers of other religions find truths in their holy texts, so do Hindus. In fact, the Vedas—written in ancient Sanskrit—are among the oldest sacred texts in existence. One can see the word 'Veda' in the name of the Vedanta school within Hinduism. The Vedas are a record of the mystical experiences of Hindu sages and the insights they arrived at. Further explanation and commentary on the Vedas appeared later, in the epics of the Mahabharata and the Ramayana. Vedanta refers to the conclusion of the Vedas. I asked Swami, "How do you think modern Hindus connect their spiritual lives with the ancient texts, such as the Mahabharata?" He tells me that not many people today actually read the full texts in their original language, but "Most Hindus are familiar with the stories." Additionally, there are retellings, so sometimes there are parts left out. Still, some things haven't changed at all. Oftentimes, young Hindus hear the stories from their elders and parents. When they are older, there is more of a focus on the written texts. Swami explains, "Besides the ethical teachings about doing good, being truthful, practicing kindness and charity, there are spiritual teachings about the nature of the soul, the purpose of life, the types of spiritual practices, etc, which Hindus try to follow in their daily life." The stories and teachings in the Vedas are certainly important in Hinduism, but Swami also believes that "A religious journey can begin with faith, but it should end with an experience."

One of the hallmarks of Hinduism is the plethora of recognized deities. Among the most recognizable are Vishnu, Shiva, Ganesh, and Saraswati. According to Swami, "Hindu deities are the manifestation of the same Supreme Being in various forms and names. They are not 'different deities' (hence, Hindus don't understand why they are called 'polytheists')—they are simply the same God appearing in different forms. Since people are different, the way they relate to God is also diverse." It has always been the case that Westerners have had a hard time identifying with Hinduism's concept of God. Those in the Abrahamic faiths only see the creator in a singular way, unless one counts all three branches' idea of a messiah. I queried Swami about the role that Hindu deities play in the guidance of humans in the additional planes of existence. He believes, "Any statement about life beyond the present one has to be accepted on faith, since no one can really 'prove' what happens after death. The only thing religious people do in every tradition is refer to their own scriptures as the source of authority. I would imagine that religious people, when they are in other planes of existence, would continue to look up to God and seek divine guidance and help in their own way." For Hindus, they expect to encounter numerous deities through their journey in the spiritual planes. It is the goal of Hindus to eventually end the cycle of reincarnation and rejoin with the Supreme Brahman, which is the original source of creation; it is above all deities, cannot be seen, and is everywhere.

Most religions, as I've discovered in my years of research, believe that humans aren't the only creatures with souls. Disagreements between the groups center around the meaning and deepness of animal souls. Hindus think that all living things hold a soul. I asked Swami, "Can people be reincarnated as animals, and what is the significance of why or why not?" He reveals that "If the mental tendencies and the karma of a soul is such as to find its best expression through an animal body rather than a human body, then the person may be reborn as an animal." The soul will go through many forms on its journey towards liberation and reunification with its original source. Swami adds, "That is another incentive Hindus have to lead noble lives, so that—if they are reborn—they will be reborn in favorable circumstances, which often includes being a human being." For many people, a long cycle of birth and death will be the norm.

Sikhism

This is the fifth-largest religion in the world (Zepps). Most of its members never left India, which is home to 90% of Sikhs. Per capita only 2% of Indians belong to this religion. Coming in second is the UK with 1.24% of its people. Lastly, 0.9% of Canadians identify themselves as being Sikhs. This is a monotheistic religion.

To gain an understanding of a belief system not well-known by most people, I travelled to the college capital of New England: Boston. I sat down with Mr. Harpreet Singh inside Harvard, the oldest university in America. Mr. Singh, PhD, graduated from the Committee on the Study of Religion at Harvard, as well as having been awarded the Certificate of Distinction in Teaching by the university. He is now a College Fellow at Harvard, in the Department of South Asian Studies. He co-founded *The Academic Room*, which is an ecosystem of professors, students, scholars, and other researchers who share information including publications, course syllabi & lectures, as well as other multimedia and can talk in discussion groups. He also co-founded the Sikh Coalition, which is the largest Sikh civil rights organization in the United States. The coalition is involved in social justice, helping those who have faced unfair treatment due to their religious affiliation, including cases involving corporations and government entities, as well as addressing hate crimes against Sikhs.

The Sikh faith first came about in the Punjab region of India over 500 years ago, and was started by Guru Nanak Dev. Singh explains that the faith is "something that grew out of dissatisfaction with the prevalent religious traditions, and Guru Nanak wanted to provide a new way of life" (Singh). Sikhs do not believe in a possible separation of religion and politics, which means that followers have a responsibility to be socially engaged and should not shy away from the realities of the miscarriage of justice. Even though the religion was born surrounded by numerous forms of Hinduism, many of the rituals found in the latter are not incorporated because they have no bearing on personal salvation with God. A commonality that is found with the Abrahamic religions is that there is one true God that is timeless and can be everywhere at once, and was self-existent before the beginning of time. Singh points out that Sikhs are true to their faith by "seeing God not pigeonholed in some sort of a specific manifestation." For instance, in Christianity, God is drawn or painted as an old man, but the Sikhs see this as not necessary and takes away from the realization of a perfect supreme being that should be seen as genderless.

In Sikhism, the belief in reincarnation and the law of karma remain from before the religion's birth. Singh mentions that if there is not a focus on a reward-filled afterlife and a home like some type of paradise, it leads Sikh believers to a realization that what they do in life now is very important. It creates an urgency for people to make a difference while living in the world. He says that with Sikhs, "even though they're a small population, if you look at what they've been able to achieve in the last 500 years is remarkable... and much of that comes from that character that is provided by a certain view of life, that you have to accomplish certain things... while you are alive... you have to worry about becoming one with God in this life." Essentially it is about having a union with God in life and not specifically *after* you die. A big part of life for Sikhs is *seva*, which in English means service. For believers, by helping others in service to humanity, they are serving God. If Sikhs fail to live up to what God expects of them in life and has bad karma, they believe that their spirit will transmigrate and reincarnate into the birth of another life in which they begin again.

When it comes to claims of people seeing ghosts, Sikhs do not see this as an aspect of life that they need to dwell on. Singh explains that while there are some mentions of mythology within the Sikh scriptures, there are no mentions specifically of ghosts. They believe that the focus on God is what is important, and what goes on in the supernatural existence created by God is nothing to be concerned with.

When it comes to physical death of Sikhs, most of them are cremated, although the scriptures which are the Guru Granth Sahib do not require that practice. Normally once a Sikh has been cremated, the ashes are put in a river or the sea. Traditionally in India or the main Sikh region of Punjab, people who have passed would be burned on a funeral pyre, but in Western countries they are brought to a crematorium. Sikhs do not mark the place that the remains were left, so there is not an inscribed stone as there is in most other religious cultures.

Depending on karma, one can experience two different realities after death, which is a common attribute among many religions.

What can be said then in the end to sum up in a spiritual sense, what it means to be Sikh? It is about becoming one with God in life, and by being in service to people in need, helping to make the world a better place.

Judaism

The Jewish religion is one of the ones in which you will find gravitating towards a particular country. The top three countries that are home to Jews based on percentage of the general public are Israel at 78%, Monaco at 2.9%, and the United States a distant third at 1.7%. Although, it should be noted that approximately 39% of all Jewish people worldwide live in the US. This is a monotheistic religion.

In my quest for knowledge about Judaic spiritual beliefs, I sought an expert who could provide a unique vantage point on this subject. One of the great strengths of Judaism is its considerable volume of texts and commentaries, both old and modern. Many rabbis and other scholars have literally devoted their lives to explaining and analyzing the Tanakh. Recently, there have been numerous books published, which deal specifically with 21st century insights and questions related to Jewish mysticism and spirituality. Of course, in all times, people have worked towards improving their understanding of how their beliefs influence their lives.

Upon browsing some of the latest book releases on topics related to Judaism, I happened across an intriguing book cover, featuring a circular rainbow, surrounding a blazing fractal-styled Star of David, which has numerous eyes embedded around the six points, and has a white light within its center. The book was *DMT and the Soul Prophecy: A New Science of Spiritual Revelation in the Hebrew Bible* (2014) by Dr. Rick Strassman. The author looks at medieval commentaries on the Hebrew Bible, prophecy and visions, Jewish metaphysics, and the effects of DMT on the brain. Strassman argues for something he calls "theoneurology", which connects the spiritual and the biological, and shows the path for the Divine to interact with people through their brains. After reading an article about this fascinating recently released title, I contacted the doctor and asked if he could take part in an interview for my own book. He graciously accepted, and I'm happy to be able to share his wealth of experience and knowledge, not only on Judaism, but also in a second interview on other aspects of his research, featured in chapter 9 of this book.

Rick Strassman, M.D., is currently Clinical Associate Professor of Psychiatry at the University of New Mexico School of Medicine. He is also President and cofounder of the Cottonwood Research Foundation, which is dedicated to consciousness research. From 1990 to 1995, he performed the first new human studies with psychedelic drugs in the

A Spirit In Motion

United States in more than 20 years, focusing on the powerful naturally occurring compound DMT. Since 1996, Dr. Strassman has been exploring models for the DMT effect focusing primarily on the Old Testament concept of prophecy.

In America, the Jewish population may be small, but in terms of its place on the world stage, it is of great importance. The relationship between the United States and Israel often features prominently in news headlines. Of course, many Jews fled Europe just before WWII got underway; while others, who survived the war, were able to escape. Many of them started new lives in America. Today, many of the American-Jewish population live in urban areas like New York City, Los Angeles, Greater Miami, Chicago, Boston, and San Francisco. Over the years, three major movements have formed in Judaism: Orthodox, Conservative, and Reform. A few others have emerged more recently.

In the 1950s and 60s, Strassman grew up in a Conservative Jewish family in the Los Angeles area. This was an important era of rebuilding for the worldwide Jewish community. I asked the doctor to tell me a bit about these early years. He recalls that the majority of his "Jewish friends belonged to the Reform stream if they belonged to any synagogue at all. Between the ages of 5 and 13, I attended six hours of Hebrew School spread out over three days per week. We learned modern Hebrew, Jewish history, culture, holidays, traditions, and read some Torah. I don't remember learning about how God took a personal role in our lives, but definitely learned that He oversaw the fate of the Jews, especially within the context of the recent birth of the nation of Israel after the Holocaust. I didn't learn much about prayer but was impressed with, but couldn't identify with, the fervor of our cantor. Our rabbi was rather stern and unapproachable. The gabbai who trained me in my haftarah for my bar mitzvah was a very devout older man who both scared me and inspired me, and I could feel his love of the tradition, although this was not really spoken about as such." Later, he went on to major in biological sciences at Stanford University, graduating in 1973.

It was around that time, as he moved towards beginning his final degree, that he became involved in Zen and meditation. He would obtain his medical degree with honors in 1977 from the Albert Einstein College of Medicine of Yeshiva University. As a university student in his early 20s, he found this path to be both intriguing and one in which he could gain first-hand experience with the meditative mind. A few decades later, he moved back towards his religious roots. He remarks, "I think those 20+ years studying and practicing Zen prepared me for reentering the stream of Jewish study. I had achieved a certain mental stability that allowed me to deal with some of the problematic issues that a superficial encounter with the Hebrew Bible reveals. In addition, the shortcomings of Buddhism could only become clear after such a long and lovingly wholehearted involvement with it. I found the answers to those shortcomings in my religious life to be in a mature rapprochement with the Jewish tradition." He had been involved with and researched psychiatry, psychopharmacology, and the function of the brain's pineal gland. The doctor's investigations of the effects of DMT in the brain took on new meaning as he considered prophetic states found in the Old Testament books.

Practically all religions believe in some form of the soul and Judaism is no exception. I asked Strassman to tell me what the soul means for the Jewish people. He explains, "I can't speak for the Jewish people, but my primary sources for understanding the Tanakh are the medieval Jewish philosophers. They were essentially neoplatonized Aristotelians who believed in the tripartite division of the soul into plant/vegetative, animal/appetitive, and human/

rational. That categorization works for me. It is only the human/rational soul that may or may not survive after death, depending on what the individual has done with his or her life. I'm not sure I agree with that, because of my theories regarding endogenous DMT. Maimonides, for example, disbelieves in animals' souls surviving after death, but it seems to me that any organism containing DMT may have access to after-death incorporeal states" (Strassman). The ideas of both Aristotle and Plato certainly affected the course of Western religious philosophy. For those who weren't philosophers, they just hoped that their belief in God and good behavior was enough to ensure a pleasant place for their soul in the afterlife. Strassman's theory goes beyond the normal conjecture about animal souls, which is covered in other parts of this book, because it presents DMT as a commonality between human and some animal brains. Obviously, the medieval thinkers he refers to did not have the opportunity to see the question of animal souls from this vantage point.

I also researched reincarnation for this book, which, historically, has not been a mainstream belief of Jews. However, as the doctor points out, the "Kabbalists and Hasidic streams believe in reincarnation, but these are later developments. There is nothing in the Torah that points to this, and the two or three references in the rest of the Tanakh are interpretable allegorically just as well as literally." Since the biblical texts are shared in one way or another between the Abrahamic religions, there are also questions raised sometimes by others about verses which may or may not allude to reincarnation. He continues, "It may be that as rational Judaism, represented by the Modern Orthodox, emerged as a viable option for Westernized Jews who wished to remain Torah-faithful but wished to eschew the 'superstition' of the traditionalism that drew the disdain of the proponents of the Jewish Enlightenment, and avail themselves of modern secular knowledge, jettisoned the idea of reincarnation in the process." Those who identify themselves as Jewish through their family, but choose not to belong to a particular sect, do not usually have a deep understanding of the philosophical analysis of the Tanakh. They also may be turned off by the more traditional sects of the faith. Strassman explains, "Jewish educators may not want to make a bad situation worse by introducing 'superstitious' ideas of reincarnation. Ironically, however, this has not prevented tens of thousands of Jews from embracing Eastern religions, and New Age and other pagan streams, in which reincarnation figures prominently." While it is clear that the concept of multiple lives is not embraced by Judaism as a whole, it may be that some younger–more liberal–Jews will give the idea more consideration than previous generations.

In Judaism, as in other religions, sin is definitely a key factor in considering one's obedience to the Creator and the state of their soul. Part of the concept of sin in Judaism is called 'cheit'. I inquired of the doctor whether this can be seen in a similar light with Christian ideas of sin or Buddhist beliefs in karma. Strassman discloses that "sin" comes with a lot of cultural and psychological baggage and that "it requires a mature and adult treatment by which we are able to separate its essence from the nonessentials." He continues, "Cheit is one of several categories of sin. I have usually seen it defined as 'missing the mark'; in other words, one is not intentionally attempting to sin but does so anyway; say, you give an overdose of antibiotics inadvertently and your patient dies. That's a sin because you killed someone who wasn't trying to kill you or kill someone else. There are other sins in this system, including sins performed inadvertently (in other words, not knowing that something was a sin), sins performed in conscious defiance of God (who the individual still does believe in), and sins performed as if there were no God at all. Each of the senses requires certain behavioral and psychological remedies." People will oftentimes make a mistake or do something wrong and then try to excuse themselves by saying "nobody's perfect". Even rabbis sin, whether they mean to or not, as we see with 'cheit'. Jewish people are expected to work on being as spiritually clean as possible and recognizant of God's laws. Strassman expands the discussion of sin by referring again to Maimonides, the 12th century Sephardic Jewish philosopher and Torah scholar, by agreeing with his sentiment that "both the moral and natural laws were created and are sustained by the same Creator and Sustainer, that being God. And those laws reflect God's wisdom and will and provide pathways for a deeper understanding, love, and obedience to Him." It is the idea that the workings of sin and redemption of the soul are part of an intentionally designed system of laws.

In terms of whether there can be a comparison to the concept of karma found in Buddhism, Strassman says, "One of the difficulties that arose during my practice and study of Buddhism was the notion that karma, or cause and effect, was without beginning and without end. But the law of karma states that everything has a beginning and an end. This led me to wonder what or who created and sustains karma, and what will exist after it. These questionings led me to the idea of God as the creator and sustainer of karma. Another question that arose in my study and practice of Buddhism was the teaching that cause and effect are impersonal. But that wasn't consistent with my own experience; that is, certain thoughts and behaviors resulted in pain and thus discouraged me from repeating them, and others resulted in pleasure or emotionally neutral states. Thus, karma discouraged some behaviors and encouraged others. For example, why would my getting angry result in my absentmindedly stubbing my toe rather than turning my backpack into a refrigerator? There seemed to be a value system inherent in cause and effect. We can explain the mechanisms of any of these outcomes, but why those outcomes are the way they are seems to reflect certain moral laws that were just as inviolable, consistent, and applicable as natural law." Through his studies of both Judaism and Buddhism, he clearly finds that there is some factor of accountability for humans and that there is a spiritual connection. However, it is also obvious that the Jewish idea of sin and the Buddhist concept of karma are two different entities and are not exactly compatible.

Many religions, Christianity included, produce an emphasis on the afterlife. I had read that Judaism is different in this regard. For Jews, the life hereafter is referred to as 'olam ha-ba', or 'the world to come'. I questioned the doctor as to why the Jewish texts spend less time on this subject than some other religions. He explains, "Maimonides teaches that there will be a messianic era after the arrival of the Messiah and during his reign the Jews will be free from the enmity of the nations and be able to study and practice mitzvot (religious rituals) to their hearts' content. All the laws of nature will remain the same, but longevity will approach that attained by the antediluvian figures in the Bible. This long period of peace would provide an opportunity for purifying their souls through study and practice for the actual olam ha ba after death when their incorporeal souls enter into a nonphysical eternal state of being in God's presence. Nachmanides, on the other hand, teaches that there is actual physical reincarnation but is less forthcoming in what happens after the death of the reincarnated body. Maimonides also posits actual physical reincarnation, but doesn't like to discuss it very much because it would lead to all manner of theoretical and/or magical speculation." Rather than pointing followers towards striving for a great afterlife filled with amazing places or things, Judaism focuses more on life here and now. Strassman calls the religion "life-affirming, not life-denying". He further expounds, "This is why discussions of the afterlife are kept to a minimum in the tradition. People are expected to work on being joyous—but in the right manner: following the Golden Rule and loving and being in awe of God. Asceticism, monasticism, self-mortification, hatred of the body and its pleasures never got much of a foothold in Judaism. One is encouraged to perfect one's soul through love of God and service to mankind. This is a joyous, not dreadful, process. And the lack of emphasis on reincarnation may be designed to keep us honest in this life, rather than giving someone the excuse that they will try harder and do better in their next life." He also told me that a lot of people automatically want to think of olam ha-ba as being the equivalent of Heaven in Christianity. However, this is not an accurate line of thought. He thinks that Jewish people, accordingly, feel the need to distance themselves from the way some others picture it. On the other hand, he points out that some Jews do find certain concepts of an eternal afterlife in spirit form, as described in varying religions, appealing.

Islam

As far as saturation goes on a country-by-country basis, Islam is the second strongest number-wise. There are thirty-three countries where 90% or more of their populations are Muslim. Indonesia holds the greatest majority of Muslims, at 12% of worldwide followers. This works out to be 88% of Indonesians. This is a monotheistic religion.

When I began my search to find an expert in this religion, I was uncertain if I'd locate that individual in my local area; the Muslim population is not prevalent where I live. In

Forever Faithful

America, the New England area is the most secular in general, but there is a small yet stable Muslim following around the greater-Boston area. However, I was pleasantly surprised when a university professor put me in touch with an authority on the matter of Islam and its beliefs in the afterlife and the soul.

I had the distinct pleasure to meet Imam Mohamed Ibrahim, Ph.D, in the Fall of 2014. The Imam, the worship leader, is the director of the Islamic Society of the Seacoast Area in New Hampshire (ISSA). The Society was formed in 1994 and incorporated in 1997 under ISNA (the Islamic Society of North America). The ISNA's mission statement is, "To foster the development of the Muslim community, interfaith relations, civic engagement, and better understanding of Islam." In 2004, ISSA was officially registered with the State of New Hampshire as an independent and non-profit organization. ISSA's Masjid (mosque) falls under the Sunni denomination of Islam; the other major branch of the religion is Shia. At the mosque there are congregational prayers and educational programs. The Imam can also officiate Islamic marriage ceremonies, funeral services, and provide off-site lectures.

Islam is one of the Abrahamic religions, meaning it is one of three major faiths that correlate the Prophet Abraham as a forefather. According to Ibrahim, the holy books of these religions, including the Qur'an, were all revealed by Allah (God). The Prophet Muhammad, born in the 6th century, was the receiver of the Qur'an. Just as Christians and Jews believe in the eternal soul and a final judgment, so do Muslims. Interestingly, Ibrahim says, "The afterlife, as a term, is not accurate." Over the years many others have agreed and used other terms, such as the 'hereafter' or the 'continued existence'. The main concepts of the soul should not conflict between those three faiths, unless the holy texts are changed by outlying sects.

A Spirit In Motion

The concept of the soul, for Muslims, is that it is born from Allah, and is singular in nature; this means that every person born has a soul and that after death, this soul survives as that single identity. The Eastern idea of reincarnation is rejected by Islam, because it is not found in the revelation, which is the Qur'an. Ibrahim explains that, for him, the foreign concept of a family member's soul going off to a new life, one who is not his or her old self, makes him feel uncomfortable. Islam holds that we each get one individual physical existence and then we just survive in spirit form.

Upon death, it is standard for Muslims to be buried rather than cremated. The soul is not asleep in the grave, but experiences an 'in-between realm'. This is known as Barzakh. The Imam explains, "The transition between death and resurrection is a distinct existence and carries with it memories and feelings." One's reality in this state will depend on what they did, or did not do, in their earthly life. For many, this means things will not be so rosy. Ibrahim says that for these people, their circumstance is the result of "lost opportunities".

The concept of good and evil can be found in varying forms in the teachings of all major religions, and Islam is no exception. Every person makes decisions while on this Earth. Some of which are regrettable. Ibrahim points out that, "Every action is accounted for." All people will be held to what they said or did. One can hope that Allah will be forgiving to them after death, but they cannot pray for him to save them after it is already too late. A deceased person's relatives can pray that Allah will have mercy on that individual. Ibrahim continued with an analogy of judgment based on balance; he says that we can envision a scale that tips based on all of the opportunities in one's life.

For all things supernatural, or beyond what we can see in our bodily lives, they can be encapsulated in what is termed the "Realm of Ghayb"; this means "the unseeable".

For instance, the Qur'an mentions there being seven layers of the heavens. Ibrahim concludes, "We don't know what these levels mean." He explains that there are various levels in both Paradise and Hell. These are rankings that guide where someone will be found based on which way their earthly life 'tipped'. However, there are undoubtedly some specifics that are simply unknown. Another topic of the unseen which sometimes elicits questions is whether 'eternal damnation' to Hell always means 'forever'. It is generally believed to mean exactly that. Yet, it is impossible for humans to really understand the concept of eternity. Ibrahim posits that this means a "very, very long time". He continues, "It is up to the grace of God. It is up to his will." In terms of the way people understand time, he says the term 'eternity' is a disincentive for people to make the wrong choices. He believes that "We should not deemphasize the deterrent." If people read that they would only be punished for one year and then get off scot-free, they would probably act recklessly, without caring.

As alluded to before, Islamic beliefs include a "Day of Reckoning" in which all people will face judgment. But before this, what gets recorded about people's lives and how does this process work? Well, Ibrahim explains that we all have angels around us. When Muslims are reading from the Qur'an and/or in a mosque, there is always an angelic presence. He says that from his own experience, "I know their existence from how I feel." Of course, angels play an important role in most major religions; they are the messengers of the Supreme Being. The Imam says that these angels dutifully record everything we do throughout our entire life! No information slips by them. If you helped an old lady cross the street, it will be recorded. On the other hand, if you become drunk and assault someone, this too will be 'written' down. When it comes time for people to own up to their actions, they will each get two "Scrolls of Deeds", one good and one bad. Most likely there will be some without shame that try to claim that the angels made mistakes in recording some of the bad deeds. However, Allah trusts his messengers and already knows the lies and excuses people may try to tell.

In Islamic theology there is a race of beings called the 'Jinn' or 'Djinn', which means the 'hidden'. Interestingly, the term 'genie' comes from a mix between 'Jinn' and 'genius'. These mysterious beings are mentioned in the Qur'an, and it says that they are one of the three self-aware creations of Allah's, along with humans and angels. It is said that we are made of clay, the angels made of light, and the Jinn from smokeless fire. They are among us, but in a different dimension. Ibrahim says, "They see us, we don't see them." They, like humans, have free will and can do both good and bad. It is natural that people would be curious about this race of creatures that occupies our 'space', but not our dimension. However, Ibrahim explains that Muslims only know for sure what the Qur'an says about the Jinn. If one believes too much in baseless speculation about these beings, it can lead to worry. He continues, "It is not healthy for us to keep thinking about that world." Many people are familiar with popular stories about individuals of all backgrounds who apparently become possessed by some invisible intelligence. There have been numerous fiction movies released in in recent decades on this topic; the most popular of these is undoubtedly *The Exorcist*. Explanations generally blame ghosts or satanic figures. Nonetheless, Muslims believe that people exhibiting signs of possession are being affected by Jinn. The Imam says we need to be careful and that "People make themselves vulnerable because they let their emotions take the best of them." The Jinn live in their realm, and we live in ours. There has always been that separation, as was intended. Ultimately, both humans and Jinn must answer to God, who knows what each race is up to at all times.

Finally, the topic of animals and their fate is often one of discussion for people of many religious backgrounds. Do animals, or any other creature for that matter, have a soul? Could they have some part in the heavenly realms? For followers of Islam, they do not need to worry themselves over these matters. Ibrahim offers the reassurance that for Allah, "Everything is accounted for." In fact, it is mentioned in the Qur'an (24:41) that Allah is praised by all life on Earth and in the heavens, including the birds of the air. The verse points out that all have their own way of prayer and praise. Ibrahim also says, "Animals are not accountable in the same way as human beings." Unlike people, they are just going on instinct and doing what comes naturally. In speaking of an old parable, he says that if two goats are butting heads in a battle, God knows the exact reason. In his own way, God will settle things between the two goats.

Christianity

According to the CIA's World Factbook, this is the largest religion in the world at 33.35% of its total population. ("Religions") There are around 2.3 billion Christians, who make up at least 90% per capita of the population of 53 countries. ("Christianity") This is a monotheistic religion.

Christianity is like looking at a leopard. As there are so many spots on the big cat, there are also a multitude of variations of the religion. The different denominations vary in customs and religious interpretation, just as the spots on a leopard are all different and are unique to each animal. The Christian sects today all came from the one who gave them life: Jesus of Nazareth. Of course, the churches became wide-spread due to Jesus' Apostles. One of the keys to understanding Christianity as a whole is to go back to the beginning of the AC era and see how it all branched out from there. Through different generations the specific customs, rituals, and biblical interpretations came into being. There are three major arms of the religion: Orthodox, Catholic, and Protestant.

Considering the multifaceted nature of Christianity in the present age, I sought to locate one who has expertise in approaching the faith from many angles. I came across a written response to University of Edinburgh Prof. Dr. Mona Siddiqui's lecture "Islamic views of Jesus". The 2014 lecture was given at Tilburg University in the Netherlands, a public research university, which is well-known for its Economics and Management School, as well as Theology. An official reaction was issued by Tilburg Prof. Dr. MJHM Poorthuis. He quite effectively compared and contrasted the lenses through which Muslims, Jews, and Christians see Jesus. In his well-rounded piece, he also talked about the unique relationship between Christians and Jews, as well as the use of the term "prophet" in connection with Mohammad and Jesus. He pointed out that both Jesus and Mary are figures who can be found within the Qur'an, a fact that is unknown to many American Christians. Through finding this response article and discovering the depth of the professor's research, I was pleased that the professor agreed to offer his insights into the world's most widespread religion, as well as its views of the spirit and the hereafter.

Prof. Dr. M.J.H.M. Marcel Poorthuis teaches inter-religious dialogue at the Tilburg School of Theology in the Netherlands. His dissertation dealt with the French-Jewish philosopher Immanuel Levinas. He has published about Catholicism, Judaism, Buddhism and recently about Dutch perceptions of Islam (From harem to fitna, Nijmegen 2011). He is also co-editor of the international book series *Jewish and Christian Perspectives* (Brill: Leiden) and chairman of the Pardes Foundation: Sources of Jewish Wisdom. His research has involved many subjects, such as the Bible & Apocrypha,

Rabbinic Judaism, Anthropology, interfaith studies and much more.

For those who are not a part of this faith, the following is a brief overview of historical points. After the ministry of Jesus and founding of the First Church of Jerusalem, a varying group of churches formed during the first few centuries. When Christians hear the word "split" in relation to their religion, they usually think of the Reformation. However, the first big break was between the Eastern and Western churches. As Poorthuis points out, the Chalcedonian churches believed in "Christ being both human and divine in two natures"; some Eastern churches, such as the Coptic and Syriac, saw Jesus' humanity and divinity as combined in one nature. There was also the issue of whether Mary had essentially given birth to God. The professor explains that this is referred to as Theotokos, and it "aimed to emphasize that Christ had been God's son from all eternity and not only adopted as his son" (Poorthuis). A group of churches called the Nestorians disagreed, which caused a further division. He says that the final split between the Eastern and Western churches (1054 AD) came down to two additional problems. The first being the "debate over the primacy of the See of Rome", which is a reference to the Pope and the overall governing body in the Vatican. Also, Poorthuis says that while the Western churches believed "that the Holy Spirit comes forth from both the Father and the Son", the Eastern churches did not. Of course, later on in the 16th century, came the Protestant Reformation. This was the separating between the Roman Catholic Church and those who disagreed on numerous points of Catholicism. Today, around half of all Christians belong to the Roman Catholic church, approximately 37% are Protestant, and the rest are mostly Eastern Orthodox ("Global Christianity").

The close connection between Judaism and Christianity may not seem extremely relevant to some today; however, it is well-known that both Jesus himself and his Apostles were Jewish. The belief in one God (many Jews write the name as 'G-d'), use of the Old Testament (Tanakh), salvation of the soul, the existence of angels & demons, and some kind of afterlife, are commonalities between the two religions. The concept of bodily resurrection was and is still shared between the two, although seen in a different light. According to the professor, "The Christians took over the idea of resurrection from Judaism, emphasizing this against gnostic and philosophical disparagement of that idea." The Gnostics saw the physical world as holding many evils, and thought of the resurrection idea as purely spiritual. Poorthuis goes on to explain that "In comparison with Judaism, the resurrection of Christ, as it were, initiated the Messianic era, whereas in Judaism resurrection remained something for the end of times." For the Jews, Jesus was not the Messiah that had been prophesied, so resurrected bodies would have to wait until the end of the world as we know it. For Christians, while they look towards having a restored physical body at some point, the sacrificial crucifixion of Jesus served to save believers from their earthly sins. The resurrection of Christ symbolizes a road to eternal salvation, rather than a certain punishment for all.

In Christianity, the salvation of an individual means the saving of his or her soul from sin through Christ. For Christians, it is a fact of life that "all have sinned and fall short of the glory of God" (Romans 3:23, NKJV). A point of contention between the various factions of the religion has been "belief and good works versus faith alone", in terms of one's outcome in the afterlife. There is sometimes disagreement over the exact purpose of Hell, and whether one could really face an eternal punishment there. Poorthuis points out that the only sticking point between Catholic and Orthodox followers is the concept of 'apokatastasis'. He describes this as "the reconciliation of everything, which implies the disappearance of evil and even of Hell". He goes on to say that "The Catholic church seems to assume that the existence of Hell is necessary to take serious radical evil, although no one is entitled to say who or whether somebody is actually in Hell." He continues, saying that the "Orthodox faith is less juridical and more cosmic in is affirmation of reconciliation of everything". There are many in the Orthodox church who believe it is possible that at the end of time, people who are within Hell, and even Satan and his minions, could be released through the grace of God. For Protestants, this could be considered blasphemous, and is certainly an unacceptable viewpoint. The progeny of the Reformation see Hell as the cost of wickedness, and for those who denied Christ as their Savior.

The belief in an in-between state called Purgatory is held by a majority of Christians, though most Protestants do not see a need for it. This type of afterlife realm is, as pointed out in other chapters of this book, a common theme with some other religions. Poorthuis weighs in on this topic by explaining that, "Purgatory is, for Protestants, loaded with the idea of deserving grace because of good works, a central point of conflict between Rome and the Reformation (Sola gratia)." Catholics feel that a goodly person who passes on can spend 'time' in Purgatory, where their soul can be healed through grace from God and prayers from loved ones in the physical world. He also points out, "The idea to pray for the dead is, however, a longstanding Christian tradition and is shared by Judaism and Islam." In addition, the professor explains that the "in-between state should not be measured with earthly ideas of time, but emphasizes that not everybody who dies is already in a fully developed religious state". Nobody knows how long someone would be in this realm because time would not be measured as it is in the physical world.

In considering the concept of Purgatory, I asked the professor if varying beliefs between some Christians on the 'ghost phenomenon' could be reconciled. Of course, the occurrence of ghost sightings is common to people in all major cultures and of various religious persuasions. Poorthuis exclaims, "Generally, Christianity is of the opinion that the dead are too much in another realm to communicate with the living. In addition, the idea of a ghostly existence does not coincide very well with the idea of a glorified body joined to the soul at resurrection." For many church leaders, the idea of a spirit-in-healing appearing to the living is perhaps undignified. Also, it would be assumed that negative spirits who did not go to Purgatory may be in Hell. However, as Poorthuis mentions, there are 'popular' contributing factors that undermine the denial of ghosts. In giving some examples, he mentions Saint Augustine, the early Christian theologian; he points out that Augustine had "to ward off the idea that the dead can be strengthened with a meal on their grave (refrigerium, a Roman idea). Nevertheless, celebrating eucharist at martyrs' graves was and is a known practice." He adds that in contemporary times, "In Mexico the commemoration of the dead happens with sharing a meal at the graves of the ancestors." There is also the well-known account from the Bible of the encounter with the witch of Endor. Saul, the first king of Israel, asked a witch to summon the spirit of Samuel, so he could query him. The king had met the witch while disguised, but she realized who he was and did not take the request lightly. She was able to bring the spirit of Samuel up from the Earth, and he appeared to Saul. The story has caused many people over the years to claim it as proof of the existence of ghosts. Detractors say this was a one-time occurrence that was allowed by the Almighty.

In looking at the topic from another angle, Poorthuis brings up the topics of demons and possessions. He goes onto explain that "The existence of demons is accepted, but is not connected with the deceased. Still, the haunting of the dead may indicate an undigested problem with the living. Exorcism is still accepted and practiced in the Catholic church, be it under strict conditions and after consulting a physician." While some Protestants may see demons in a 'superstitious' fashion, the professor says that the "fear of demons seems to be strongest in Protestant fundamentalist circles". These are all things that would be referred to as paranormal, and opinions certainly vary. For those who are sure they have seen a spirit possession, or ghosts in their home, they already know what they believe. Perhaps some things will 'officially' remain a mystery.

5

Darkness, Grey, and Light

> "My restless, roaming spirit would not allow me to remain at home very long."[7]
>
> - BUFFALO BILL

ONE COULD describe the dimension of Hell as being in the belly of the beast. It is the destination that no one wants to go to, and the place that only the foolishly bold claim they are going. In all great civilizations over the years, a punishment beyond bodily life has been a staple of religious belief. Many times, people believe that they stand for good; their enemy represents evil, and of course this means they must be going to Hell.

The various names that different religions use for describing the "middle dimension" and for the "lake of fire" get mixed up and people confuse them. Most of the major

---

[7] "The Life" (See Bibliography)

religions teach that there are levels of Hell which coincide with how sinful a person has been in their earthly life. The major difference between religions that believe in "hell realms" is that some see it as a temporary stay, while others do not. For followers of Islam, banishment is forever, but in Buddhism for example, it is but one stop. There are mainly two ways we can read about the hell concept. The first is in the official scriptures of the world's major religious groups. The second are books, papers, or quotes from figures throughout history concerning their opinions and educated guesses.

In the ancient poem *The Odyssey*, Ulysses and his men were beginning to see the reality of the underworld when a so-called phantom-prophet explained that "this is thy life to come, and this is fate…". As Ulysses begins his regretful tour, he exclaims, "Swarms of spectres rose from deepest hell, With bloodless visage, and with hideous yell. They scream, they shriek; and groans and dismal sounds stun my scared ears, and pierce hell's utmost bounds" (Homer). This was Hades, ruled by the god of the same name; it was an influence later on for Christian theologians who framed their view of Hell and Satan. In Homer's time, it was understood that almost all people, even decent people, would have to face the underworld. A small minority, made up of ultimate heroes and those seen as demigods, would go straight to Heaven.

Eastern Views

For Buddhists, Hindus, and Sikhs, Hell is called Naraka, and like Western religions, the majority believes there are different levels or areas. For many people in these faiths, the Catholic concept of Purgatory is embodied in Naraka, although in comparison it would most likely be the least harsh level for Catholics. In Hinduism, bad karma is eventually expiated. The Merriam-Webster dictionary defines expiation as "the act of making atonement." The descriptions of flames, horrible punishments, and hell-beings are similar to most Western interpretations of Hell. There are some sects of the aforementioned religions that view Naraka as a private hell which emanates from the individual instead of an actual shared dimension that others see also. It is more similar across the major religious groups than ideas of heaven.

In 1910, the book *Sacred Writings: Part Two* was published. It is the 45th volume of the Harvard Classics series. Its editor was Charles William Eliot, who had retired the year prior from being President of Harvard University; he served in that position for 40 years, longer than any other, before or since. The book was a helpful resource, especially to American college students, because this was an opportunity to read eastern religious texts in the student's own language. There are four religions that are covered in this volume: Christianity, Islam, Hinduism, and Buddhism. In a section under Buddhism entitled "Death's Messengers", translated from the Anguttara Nikaya text, it is explained what will happen to people who have focused their lives on doing evil things: "Having done evil with his body, done evil with his voice, and done evil with his mind, he arrives after the dissolution of the body, after death, at a place of punishment, a place of suffering, perdition, hell. Then, O priests, the guardians of hell seize him by the arms at every point, and they show him to Yama, the ruler of the dead, saying, 'Sire, this man did not do his duty to his friends, to his parents, to the monks, or to the Brahmans, nor did he honor his elders among his kinsfolk. Let your majesty inflict punishment upon him'" ("Buddhism"). The text makes it clear that an individual with bad karma will not get to slip by unnoticed. In this passage, the guardians allude to the idea that people have many responsibilities in life, and should be considering others around them.

In the latter part of *Sacred Writings: Part Two*, the Hindu perspective on the afterlife is detailed in "Hinduism: The Book of the Separateness of the Divine and Undivine". In chapter sixteen of the Bhagavad Gita, one of the central texts of the Hindu religion, the great warrior archer Arjuna is asking questions of Krishna; who is one of the embodiments of Vishnu, the Supreme God. Krishna talks of the righteous, but then says he wants to speak of those he calls "the Unheavenly"; he says these people have the traits of deceitfulness, arrogance, pride, quickness to anger, harsh and evil speech, and ignorance. In a sub-section of the chapter called "ensnared", Krishna speaks of the hard truth that awaits arrogant people who are rich and powerful in the Earthly world;

> Slaves to their passion and their wrath, they buy wealth with base deeds, to glut hot appetites; "Thus much, to-day," they say, "we gained! thereby such and such wish of heart shall have its fill; and this is ours! and th' other shall be ours! To-day we slew a foe, and we will slay our other enemy tomorrow! Look! Are we not lords? Make we not goodly cheer? Is not our fortune famous, brave, and great? Rich are we, proudly born! What other men live like to us? Kill, then, for sacrifice! Cast largesse, and be merry!" So they speak darkened by ignorance; and so they fall–tossed to and fro with projects, tricked, and bound in net of black delusion, lost in lusts–down to foul Naraka. (871)

Darkness, Grey, and Light

Western Views

The Catholic Church teaches that there is an area of the afterlife called Limbo, and that it is negative rather than positive. The concept that there are varying degrees of the afterlife experience is common to most religions. A lot of people explain this mindset by saying that God is just, so that every person is not lumped together in one outcome. The most widely read fictional book about Hell is certainly *Dante's Inferno*, written by Dante Alighieri in the first quarter of the 14th century. The proliferation of the book in its English translation came about in the latter half of the 19th century. Just as it is with the Holy Bible, there have been various translations over the years as the use of language changes with the times. Dante's book has had a profound influence over the centuries since its completion on how people conceptualize a negative afterlife. It would be a reasonable argument that the book, with its terrifying details of Hell, actually assisted the Catholic Church in quantifying some of its teachings. In canto four of the book, Dante says that the first circle of Hell is Limbo, and it is the beginning of an abyss at the edge of a valley.[8]

It states that the people in the first level are ones who led good lives regardless of their religion, but were never baptized and considered fully Christian. This type of thinking was in line with the teaching of the Catholic Church at the time. To illustrate the various levels of Hell in the book, the author finds different famous people in the underworld such as Cleopatra, Saladin, and Brutus. After the first circle of Hell, Dante pictures an evil creature called Minos, who sifts through people's sins and decides what level they will go to. Dante states in canto five, "Minos waits awful there and snarls, the case examining of all who enter in; and, as he girds him, dooms them to their place. I say, each ill-starred

---

[8] A canto is Italian for a division between chapters in an epic poem.

spirit must begin on reaching him its guilt in full to tell; and he, omniscient as concerning sin, sees to what circle it belongs in Hell" (Alighieri). Those souls arriving in this place of torment will not have a say as to their fate.

To get insight into what could happen to condemned souls, we can read a Christian perspective from a Protestant Bible. In Matthew 25 (verses 31-33, 41, & 46), it says, referring to the second coming of Jesus:

> When the Son of Man comes in his glory, and all the angels with him, he will sit on his glorious throne. All the nations will be gathered before him, and he will separate the people one from another as a shepherd separates the sheep from the goats. He will put the sheep on his right and the goats on his left... Then he will say to those on his left, "Depart from me, you who are cursed, into the eternal fire prepared for the devil and his angels..." Then they will go away to eternal punishment...

This is an outcome which, according to Protestant leaders, should come to no surprise, as the Revelation story has been known for 2,000 years. The belief that humans have free will and must answer for their sins seems to be an equalizer.

In his book "Fundamentals of the Faith", author Peter Kreeft offers up essays in Christian Apologetics, with the intent of explaining the logic behind the Christian faith. Kreeft, a Catholic, is also a longtime professor in the philosophy department at Boston College. Over time, it has been a common practice for Christian leaders to press the need for salvation, oftentimes by stressing the belief that without it, one's soul will undoubtedly be destined for eternal despair. The author touches upon the importance of this aspect of teaching by explaining, "Sure, we'll be mocked as vindictive, manipulative, or fundamentalist. Let it be so. Sometimes it seems that we're more afraid of sharing our Lord's holy unrespectability than of hell itself. It's a small price to pay for the salvation of a single infinitely precious soul. And that is the business we're supposed to be in" (Kreeft). A commonality between Catholic, Protestant, and Orthodox churches is the belief that every person is loved by God, and that if only one individual is considered saved in a church service or event, then it was worth the effort.

In the Islamic faith, the realm of misery is called Jahannam.[9] It is fairly similar to descriptions of it which came centuries earlier from other Abrahamic religions. Most Muslims believe that the majority of humanity will spend time here due to the heaviness of their corruption and bad decisions. There is currently not a complete consensus on whether all those people will spend eternity there, or if some of them could eventually be released; it is often said that it is ultimately up to Allah to decide the fate of all. Those ending up in this realm must deal with fire and harsh treatment. There are nineteen guardians of Jahannam who are led by one called Maalik. They are referred to in the scriptures of Islam. According to Sura 43:78 of the Qur'an, desperate souls pleaded with Maalik, but he said the condemned had been given the truth and most did not want it.

In his fairly recent article "Islam's Understanding of Hell", Dr. Faheem Younas, a Muslim clinical associate professor at the University of Maryland, argued that Jahannam should not be interpreted as being a place of eternal punishment. He acknowledges that there are many ideas today of what Hell is supposed to be. As a doctor, he believes we should "Think of hell as a hospital where sick souls belonging to any religion will be admitted for, not punishment, but treatment, albeit a painful one" (Younus). He claims that

---

[9] Also referred to as Jaheem (The Fierce Fire), Al-Hawiyah (The Pit), Sa'eer (The Burning Fire), and others.

souls go through a 'cleansing' period. Using the word 'guilty' in association with souls, he also compares Hell to a jail. The doctor points to hadith works which indicate an eventual release of all of these souls.[10] While he acknowledges the many acts which, as the Prophet mentioned, advance one towards Hell, Younas presents a passage from the Qur'an (9:157) in which Allah says, "I will inflict my punishment on whom I will. But My mercy encompasses all things." He says it is only a matter of time before our views change on the question of an eternal Hell. However, for the more conservative leaders of Islam, this may seem unlikely.

If you've ever been in a room alone and felt like someone was there watching you, you may have been right. What you might not have realized, though, was that it could be a ghost, and that it may feel trapped. It could be stuck in the middle dimension for a time, or earthbound as some call it, and there could be various reasons for it. What is tying it to a certain area of our physical world, but seen through its dimension, are experiences from its life or the circumstance of its death. Regardless of whatever the ghost is doing, it is in the middle dimension which simply overlaps the surface of the earth, at least the top part of it. Imagine if every airline flight was that close, everyone would be flying instead of driving! In fact there have been a number of ghost investigations from popular shows on television where a team member asks something like "where are you" and they get a reply via EVP that says "I'm here." The ghost is practically hitting the investigators over the head with a frying pan, trying to say that it is standing right next to them. There are probably many ghosts who find themselves in the company of the

---

[10] Texts which refer to the teachings and sayings of the Prophet Muhammed.

Darkness, Grey, and Light

living and try to communicate with them somehow, but many times the living do not realize it.

In Luke 16:19-31, the story of the rich man and a beggar named Lazarus, who was hanging around at the gate of the man's home, is told. To really understand the story we must look at the entire account:

> There was a rich man who was dressed in purple and fine linen and lived in luxury every day. At his gate was laid a beggar named Lazarus, covered with sores and longing to eat what fell from the rich man's table. Even the dogs came and licked his sores. The time came when the beggar died and the angels carried him to Abraham's side. The rich man also died and was buried. In Hades, where he was in torment, he looked up and saw Abraham far away, with Lazarus by his side. So he called to him, "Father Abraham, have pity on me and send Lazarus to dip the tip of his finger in water and cool my tongue, because I am in agony in this fire." But Abraham replied, "Son, remember that in your lifetime you received your good things, while Lazarus received bad things, but now he is comforted here and you are in agony. And besides all this, between us and you a great chasm has been set in place, so that those who want to go from here to you cannot, nor can anyone cross over from there to us." He answered, "Then I beg you, father, send Lazarus to my family, for I have five brothers. Let him warn them, so that they will not also come to this place of torment." Abraham replied, "They have Moses and

> the Prophets; let them listen to them." "No, father Abraham," he said, "but if someone from the dead goes to them, they will repent." He said to him, "If they do not listen to Moses and the Prophets, they will not be convinced even if someone rises from the dead."

So, essentially, the rich man who thinks very highly of himself in life is really no better off than the homeless beggar, but in this case worse off. Clearly Abraham says that spirits cannot travel from his side, also known as "Abraham's Bosom," to Hades or vice versa, that once they are in one or the other that is where they stay. Abraham is also saying that even if a ghost appears to the living and/or communicates to them about the truth of life after death, they will not necessarily believe or put faith in it. However, it could be interpreted that "rises from the dead" could mean that the actual body would come back to life. It should be stated also that it says in the Holy Bible that, after Jesus Christ rose again, he took the spirits of the righteous with him up to heaven during his ascension. Even though the distance between the rich man and Abraham was 'far away', they could still see each other. Thus, there seems to be an implied layer in-between heaven and hell. This is a controversial viewpoint, which not everyone agrees with. The idea that Abraham was secured away somewhere 'above' Hell, but below Heaven, originates with the stories indicating that, at that time, Heaven was not yet open to humanity.

In Hinduism and Buddhism there is a dimensional plane called peta-loka. This is the base layer representing the planet's surface, it is the astral plane, but we cannot see it as physical humans. This realm is within the kāma-loka sphere, the world of desire or "sensory gratification". This is the home of ghosts. Some people relate this to the Catholic concept of Purgatory. The Catholic Church generally teaches that Purgatory is meant as a way to heal the effects of sin on the person's soul, rather than taking away the sin itself. For Buddhists and Hindus, peta-loka is generally for those who were decent people, but had a strong attachment to something or someone in the physical world. This could be a rich person who loves their mansion and sports car, or a person who is jealous that his or her ex is with someone else, or one whose life was all about wanting to make more money.

In 2001 a free e-book entitled *The 31 Planes of Existence* was released through the Buddha Dharma Education Association Inc. They partnered with the Mahindarama Buddhist (Sri Lanka) Temple in Penang, Malaysia. The book contains teachings by the late Venerable Bhante Ācāra Suvanno Mahāthera, who was a monk there at the temple. He said that people's karma in life will direct them to the appropriate plane in the afterlife; the status of their karma around the time of their death, what it became in the end, will determine where their next stop is after the first plane following death. He believed there are other universes, and that there is other life in the universe; this 31 plane afterlife exists for all life-forms. Mahāthera talked about the human ghosts within the peta-loka realm which overlaps our own dimension. While there are certainly troubled ghosts, the monk also said, "I think that friendly ghosts exist in this realm too, the ones who have lost their way, or those who died suddenly and don't know that they're dead yet or who have 'unfinished business' to do. For these 'trapped' beings, *mettā* (loving-kindness) from us will help them along; there's no need to be afraid of ghosts" (Mahāthera).

One of the common questions that comes up regularly on internet message boards is "where does someone go in the afterlife if they do not know about religious icons such as Buddha, Jesus, Muhammad, or Krishna?" Most of the world population believes in at least one of these figures, or another one. From their perspective, there are specifics on entry into the afterlife and ultimate destinations. What about an African tribe member who lives in a remote area who has never met an outsider? Now every year that goes by this becomes less likely, but this has been used as an example over the centuries. In a similar situation, members of a tribe might hunt an animal that a first world country thinks is becoming an endangered species, but to them, they are just procuring food to survive. The answer to the question, predictably, is that it depends on the religion of the one answering. There are some who believe that indigenous peoples will go straight to the middle dimension and ultimately move to a final destination based on what Hindus would call karma because they recognized an overall creator. This is, however, not necessarily a mainstream belief. A common explanation of this notion is based on the assumption that there is a fair and loving creator.

The concept of an in-between realm, as mentioned above, is one that has been around for many centuries. Of course there have been reports of ghosts for thousands of years. According to *US Catholic* online, in reference to that branch of Christianity, the "church formulated the doctrine of Purgatory at the Councils of Florence and Trent in the 15th and 16th centuries. The catechism defines purgatory as a 'final purification of the elect, which is entirely different from the punishment of the damned'" (Townsend). Unlike Protestant leaders of the day, the Catholic members of these pivotal councils made it clear that they believed the movement of souls in the afterlife was broader in scope. The Protestant Reformation had been going on around this time, starting around 1517, which offered Christians a different approach to the faith. Leaders of the Reformation included Martin Luther and John Calvin. Their disagreements with the powerful Roman Catholic Church were numerous; they had problems with the figurehead and power of the Pope, the selling of indulgences,[11] the idea that salvation through faith in Christ was all that was needed (that works were not a requirement), the over-abundant focus on Mary, the issue of marriages for priests (which the Catholics outlawed), the sometimes shady connections between the Church and state leaders, and the existence of Purgatory (Protestants did not believe it necessary).

The Council of Trent was convened between 1545 and 1563, and was formed in response to the Protestant affront. It was an opportunity to make clear what the Catholic Church believed. According to the late Father John A. Hardon, a Catholic author and lecturer, the council members made a special decree for the topic of Purgatory (Hardon). Father Hardon made the point that the Church had incorporated the teaching of Purgatory all along. He referred to this particular declaration:

> Whereas the Catholic Church, instructed by the Holy Ghost, has, from the sacred writings and the ancient tradition of the Fathers, taught, in sacred councils, and very recently in this ecumenical Synod, that there is a Purgatory, and that the souls there detained are helped by the suffrages of the faithful, but principally by the acceptable sacrifice of the altar; the holy Synod enjoins on bishops that they diligently endeavor that the sound doctrine concerning Purgatory, transmitted by the holy Fathers and sacred councils, be believed, maintained, taught, and every where proclaimed by the faithful of Christ. But let the more difficult and subtle questions, and which tend not to

---

[11] When a parishioner would pay a fee to the church that was supposed to clear past sins, or let them skip Purgatory.

edification, and from which for the most part there is no increase of piety, be excluded from popular discourses before the uneducated multitude. (Luebke)

The question of whether Purgatory is in fact a reality is something which will, most likely, never be settled between Catholics and Protestants. However, the two sects do agree upon the two final outcomes for spirits in the afterlife: Heaven or Hell. Today, the afterlife beliefs of Catholics are similar to Protestants, but many parishioners hold a relaxed viewpoint. As far as discussion of ghosts, related to Purgatory, the official church standpoint is vague. Many Christians, regardless of sect, are at least open to the possibility of the existence of ghosts.

The road to Heaven runs through the light, and the toll is death. While the toll seems high, the destination makes it all worth it. The Muslims call it Jannah, the Christians Heaven, the Jews Shamayim, the Buddhists Deva-gati, the Hindus Svarga Loka, & the Sikhs Sachkhand. It has had many names over the centuries and has been a part of the beliefs of almost all cultures.

If you look at the concept of Heaven, and condense it to a single thought, you end up with an exclusively positive existence in pure spirit form. When analyzing the different religions, one will find many similarities in the telling of what Heaven(s) is. However, once you get beyond the most basic details, then you begin to see divergences. However, this begs the question, "Are there actually various heavens?" Let's look at a–possibly blasphemous–analogy of sorts. When people talk about going on vacation to Disney World, they generally have a similar idea of what that means. There are restaurants, hotels, outdoor productions, fire-

Darkness, Grey, and Light

works, costumed figures, amusement rides, etc. It could be assumed that if two unconnected visitors arrived at this tourist destination on the same day, that they'd have access to all the same experiences. Of course, this doesn't mean they have all the same interests as the other person. If one of the visitors was a tourist from another country and wasn't familiar with one of the costumed movie characters, that individual will not see the costumed actor the same way as the person who has that familiarity. If both visitors went back home and described to friends what Disney World is, there would be variances in the explanations.

Inevitably, the concept that a heavenly existence could be approached differently draws upon religion. Though, for atheists, it is a moot point. The Greek Stoic philosopher known as Epictetus, born a few decades after the death of Jesus, generally believed in God and Heaven. His ideas were put into books, including *The Discourses*, compiled by his student Flavius Arrian. Later on, the former student would work under the rule of the popular Roman Emperor Hadrian (Seddon). Within the philosopher's recorded teachings, he is quoted as saying, "All religions must be tolerated... for every man must get to heaven in his own way." Just as it is today, in Epictetus' time there were numerous organized religions, which often conflicted with one another. As a great thinker, he was open to consider many possibilities in his search for truth. For Epictetus, a path to Heaven, which stood alone, may have been too narrow. In the larger picture, he decided that one cannot change the events that lead to one's destiny and must be able to capitulate to it. He also said that people are accountable for their actions and that it is our charge to help others. If one was able to follow these ideas, while being both conscientious and in harmony with nature, then true happiness would find him or her.

One of the greatest influences on later Western religion & philosophy and the concept of the heavens was the Greek civilization. They believed, as those in the East did, that there were a multitude of gods who had power over humanity; these divine beings came from realms above the Earth, where the stars shined bright. Those studying astronomy and philosophy posited that there were spheres which enclosed the planet, so that each one was inside of another. These spheres would expand outward to the very perimeter of the Universe. This outer area was not reachable by mere humans, but was only home to the divine. Today, many of the religious still think of Heaven as being *up* and that this realm(s) has actual levels, like in a building.

Jannah of Islam

Many Muslims believe there are seven levels of Jannah. The usual translation of the word means "the garden." It is probably not a coincidence that there are NDE stories from Muslims and people of other religions that see a garden paradise. It is written in the Qur'an "O soul who is at rest, return to thy Lord, well-pleased with Him, well-pleasing Him. So enter among My servants, and enter My garden" (89:27-30). There are descriptions in the holy book that mention trees, plants, rivers, lakes, and an overall splendid landscape. Souls can experience this serenity in varying levels, so long as they have earned it.

In the end, Muslims are really striving to reach Paradise. Just as those from other religions read descriptions of this place, followers of Islam must picture it in their minds. The brilliance of Paradise, in reality, is said to be much greater than one can fathom. Upon arriving in Jannah, a Muslim would find great happiness, with the greatest joy coming from a closer bond with Allah. Those who find themselves in Paradise after bodily death must have had real faith in Allah, as well as his messenger Muhammad ("Credo").

Darkness, Grey, and Light

Heaven of Christianity

A lot of Christians believe there are seven levels of Heaven. Most Christians see it as being a shining city which has gates, only allowing in the select. Most sects agree that those allowed in have accepted that Jesus Christ died for humanity's sins on the cross. There is a description in the Bible of the actual city and how it appears. There is also a garden paradise associated with Heaven, as there is with Islam. Many Christians who have had an NDE talk about visiting a garden area and seeing people they know from their physical life who've passed away.

Christians look forward to this dimension as their final resting stop in an eternal life. People expect to be reunited with many of their family and friends, and that it will bring them great joy. Followers expect there to be beautiful harmonious music played, learning of information concealed during bodily life, the absence of fear and doubt, and the opportunity to interact with Jesus and the Apostles.

Shamayim of Judaism

Many Jewish people believe there are seven levels of Shamayim. Compared to all other major religions, with the exception of Sikhism, the Jewish texts do not extensively discuss the heavenly realm. In a 2005 interview with Barbara Walters for ABC News, Rabbi Neil Gillman, a philosophy professor at New York's Jewish Theological Seminary, talked about Jewish afterlife beliefs. He said, "For the past 2,000 years, most Jews believed that at death the body and the soul separate, the body is interred and disintegrates in the Earth, the soul goes off to be with God. At the end of days, God will resurrect bodies, will reunite body and soul, and the individual will come before God to account for his or her life" (Walters). This is essentially the same teaching as is found in Christianity.

The Jewish people are generally more focused on the type of life they live on Earth, rather than what will happen to them in the afterlife. According to *JewFAQ* online, "The spiritual afterlife is referred to in Hebrew as Olam Ha-Ba (oh-LAHM hah-BAH), the World to Come, although this term is also used to refer to the messianic age. The Olam Ha-Ba is another, higher state of being" (Rich). Unlike Christians, the Jewish people do not expect a welcoming to Shamayim by Jesus, because they do not regard him as the savior. This is what is meant by the term "messianic age". They believe that there will be a future messiah who will be sent to Earth by the creator.

Deva-gati of Buddhism

The subject of Heaven within Buddhism, from a Western point-of-view, is hard to grasp. One of the major differences between this Eastern religion and others is that one cannot stay in the heavenly realm for eternity. There are three realms of Heaven in Buddhism. Within those are twenty-eight heavens. Some say there are thirty-three. Karmaloka (The realm of desire includes six areas). Rupaloka (The realm of form includes eighteen areas). Arupaloka (The realm of formlessness includes four areas) (Yun). The different heavens are not the same, and are not equal. Deva-gati is what one might call the premier area that one would move up to before being able to break free from the cycle of birth, life, and death. Beyond the concept of the heavenly realms, the state of being called Nirvana is the end goal.

The unique offering to world conceptions of the afterlife from Buddhism is Nirvana, according to Rev. Kusala Ratna Karuna, who is a resident monk at the International Buddhist Meditation Center in Los Angeles. He says, "Nirvana is the end of suffering while you are alive and the end of rebirth after you die" (Karuna). Some of the early concepts of the religion were borrowed from Hinduism by Buddha, for instance, the idea that there are multiple areas or levels of heaven. It is written that time is much different in heaven, that if you spend one day there, a whole 400 years will go by on the Earth! Karuna says some people will spend many thousands of years in heaven and then they will either be born into a new body or experience Nirvana, never having a human body again.

Svarga Loka of Hinduism

Most Hindus acknowledge there are seven upper areas, or Lokas. Once you remove the earth's surface as the first, you are then actually just left with six. They believe that once you die you go here to get what you deserve based on your karma, of the good and bad things you have done in your human life. If you need much improvement still, Hindus believe you will be reincarnated into a new life. If, however, you are of pure heart and ready to advance in the Lokas, you can move towards the top of the heavenly worlds to end your journey by joining Brahman, the creator god.

Svarga is where deserving souls go to reside in a paradise, before they have to move on to reincarnate. The individuals who have made it to this realm have been faithful and did positive things for others, but are not ready to be released from the cycle of life and death. If they are able to attain liberation later on, they will go to the supreme realm; it is ruled over by Lord Vishnu, an avatar of Brahman, the Supreme Lord ("Svarga").

A Spirit In Motion

Sachkhand of Sikhism

The end goal of Sikhs is Sachkhand, in which the physical human journey is over and they are in the presence of God for eternity. This concept is fairly different than western religious views of the final stop in the spiritual world. According to *RealSikhism* online, "If you meditate on God and purify your soul by getting rid [of] lust, anger, greed, attachment, and ego, you merge back with God and your cycle of life and death is gone forever. The other one is that if you do not worship God and realize Him, you will be reincarnated" ("What happens"). There are other possibilities as well, such as being positioned in good human reincarnations, if one needs a little more work to better their soul. For some, life and death will be like an aimless desert trek.

6

The Art of Death

> "Art washes away from the soul
> the dust of everyday life."[12]
>
> - PABLO PICASSO

THE NEED to express one's way of seeing the world is inherent to humanity. One of the most obvious ways of showing ideas to others is through artwork. Archeologists tell us that some of the very first art was crudely painted on to rock walls by cave dwellers thousands of years ago. As time went on, cultures around the world depicted all types of subjects in their artistry, such as animals, farming, gods, wars, and even life after death. Religion has certainly been a popular focus for many artists, from the ancient Hindus, to the Egyptians, through Medieval Europe, to contemporary times. Some of the most fasci-

---

[12] "Famous" (See Bibliography)

nating creations have drawn on religious beliefs of good versus evil, caring or angry gods, rewards contrasted with punishments, as well as lives reborn.

The ancient Egyptian civilization was one of the greatest empires the world has ever seen. Yet, with such a great focus on creating grand architecture, the people were just as concerned with the world beyond. With the excavations of the tombs of the pharaohs, some of the most intriguing 'treasures' found inside have actually been the wall art. The many illustrations represent parts of funerary texts. One of these texts was called the 'Amduat', which is said to mean "That Which Is In the Afterlife". This 'book' talks about the travels of the Sun god 'Ra' in the afterlife, which it says he made using his solar boat in-between the setting and rising of the Sun (Dunn). Artistic depictions from the Amduat are found in tombs of kings such as Ramesses III, who held power in the 20th dynasty; the pharaoh died in 1155 BC. The pharaohs believed they would merge with Ra. In one of the engraved wall illustrations in his tomb, the Sun god Ra as seen "in ram-headed form is accompanied by other gods" (Underwood). In the depiction, the gods are all standing lined up on the boat, with the Sun god in the middle. Apparently the major illustration was set first, with hieroglyphs added afterwards, due to the glyphs being 'wrapped' above. One of the inherent artistic virtues of Egyptian writing is the actual hieroglyphic symbols themselves. The 'ankh', which is a symbol that commonly represents eternal life, appears numerous times in the artwork. In similarity to other tomb wall art, the main paint colors used are gold, teal, green, brown and red. The fact that much of the Egyptian wall art lies underground has been beneficial in terms of preservation.

Moving forward some 1,200 years, the greatness of Egypt was over and the presiding authority was the Western Roman Empire. The seat of power was now on the other

The Art of Death

side of the great Mediterranean Sea, stretching from the border of the Middle East to the Atlantic Ocean. The Western Roman Empire started with the defeat of the Ptolemaic Kingdom in 31 BC and the deaths of Cleopatra and Mark Antony. During the late 1st century till the end of the 2nd century AD, there were a succession of leaders who are known today as the "Five Good Emperors". This phrase originated from the famous political philosopher Niccolò Machiavelli in 1503.[13] He had the following to say about the five adopted emperors:

> From the study of this history we may also learn how a good government is to be established; for while all the emperors who succeeded to the throne by birth, except Titus, were bad, all were good who succeeded by adoption, as in the case of the five from Nerva to Marcus. But as soon as the empire fell once more to the heirs by birth, its ruin recommenced... Titus, Nerva, Trajan, Hadrian, Antoninus, and Marcus had no need of praetorian cohorts, or of countless legions to guard them, but were defended by their own good lives, the good-will of their subjects, and the attachment of the senate. ("Nerva-Antonine")

During the rule of Antoninus Pius (138-161 AD), religion in the empire was multifaceted; there was a mix of worship of state-approved gods, cults, Judaism, as well as the fairly new disruption called Christianity. At first the state saw the Christian followers as a cult. In an ironic twist, after the fall of the Western Roman Empire, the eastern half

---

[13] The general consensus from experts on Machiavelli is that he was not a religious man, but rather that he espoused the need for organized religion in republics, because they aided in both a civic and moral fashion.

would become Christian ("The Roman"). In a process called 'apotheosis', many Roman emperors upon their death would become recognized by the state as gods. Around this time the use of 'stelae', or engraved stone death monuments, was common. In explaining the importance of these Roman stelae in her 1915 book *Apotheosis and After Life: Three Lectures on Certain Phases of Art and Religion in the Roman Empire*, author Eugenie Sellers (Mrs. Arthur Strong) said the following:

> By the second century A.D. the sepulchral art of the Roman Empire was everywhere in possession of a rich imagery, but nowhere better than on the provincial stelae can we follow the spiritual ideals that were spreading from the East to the Western provinces of the Empire. Like that of the Christian tombs of a somewhat later date, their iconography is an illuminating commentary on the beliefs of the time. However crude their symbolism, however naive their images or rude their art, these stelae consistently offer to the living the supreme guarantee that death is not irrevocable. Their distinctive note is the defiance of death, the assertion of life beyond the grave. (Strong)

From current-day analysis, it appears that Emperor Antoninus Pius was generally respected by most Romans. There were previous rulers, of course, who were known for tyranny and cruelness. According to the *Illustrated History of the Roman Empire* online, Antoninus was thoughtful and had compassion for others, even for abused slaves. At the end of his life, the emperor handed the reins of power over to his adopted son Marcus Aurelius. When the Roman Senate

The Art of Death

decided to grant Antoninus divine status, none of its members objected. Aurelius, in memorializing his adoptive father, exclaimed, "Remember his qualities, so that when your last hour comes your conscience may be as clear as his" ("Antoninus").

During the reign of Aurelius with his co-emperor Lucius Verus, they commissioned a marble column on a base, which honored their progenitor. The inscribed base, now missing the column, can be found today at the Vatican Museum. The most prominent of the four sides features the deceased emperor, as well as his wife, who is known as Faustina the Elder. On the lower right sits Roma, a goddess who represents Rome, as she seems to bid farewell to the couple. Antoninus and his wife are lifted to heaven by a large winged spiritual being. Also assisting them are two eagles on either side (Sullivan). The symbolism of the eagles, according to Dr. Nigel Pollard in a BBC discussion of the Roman Imperial cult, was "associated with imperial power and Jupiter - and were typically released during imperial funerals to represent the spirits of the deceased" (Pollard). In contemporary times the idea of a nation's leader depicted posthumously as a god would seem absurd, but in the Roman Empire it was just business as usual.

Far to the east, around five centuries later, one of the greatest series of art projects ever seen would be launched; it would be added to for at least 600 years! There was even a small amount of final work done between the 15th and 19th centuries. The Dazu Rock Carvings in south-western Chongqing, China, were first started in the 7th century during the Tang Dynasty. Although, things really got rolling two centuries later. The carvings are made up of around 50,000 statues, and are based on Buddhism, Confucianism and Taoism. The collection as a whole was recognized in 1999 as a "World Heritage Site" by UNESCO. With the large number of artists who contributed over the years, the range

A Spirit In Motion

of styles and subject matter make the site one of the richest locations for eastern religious art. The Dazu Rock Carvings are fairly popular with tourists from around the world, who are frequently driven in from the city on buses.

Of the thousands of carvings across many miles of historic sites, some of the most impressive pieces can be found in the Baoding Shan section. The man who was largely responsible for the roughly 10,000 statues in this area was Zhao Zhifeng. According to historian and China expert Ross Terrill, in his 1990 *New York Times* article, "Serene Haven of Buddhist Art", monk Zhifeng had individual figures and group pieces made. The carvings, under his direction, were produced for more than 70 years. The concepts had a connection with the Buddhist philosophy taught at his own school nearby. Terrill toured the site in 1990 while working on his book *China On My Mind*. In observing one of the most prolific displays, referred to as the "Hell Tribunals and Punishments", he recalled that "wrongdoers are hung from hooks, boiled in oil, put out to die of cold" (Terrill). He also noted figures being attacked with sharp weapons. There are four major rows in this large artwork. As is pointed out by the *Woodenfish Project* online, which "aims to build a bridge between East Asian Buddhism and young people from around the world through education", the top two rows include figures which dole out the proper justice on those who have died. They go on to say that "In the middle of this section we find a huge image of the Bodhisattva Ksitigarbha, who is believed to be the only one who can save the deceased from a gruesome destiny" (Gauvain). For those familiar with some of the paintings of hellish scenes from the later Renaissance period, these Buddhist depictions are somewhat similar.

Another highlight of the Baoding Shan collection of statues is the "Wheel of Reincarnation", also referred to as the "Transmigration in the Six Ways". It is a roughly 25-

The Art of Death

foot tall sculpture of the demon Mara clutching a large wheel showing the path of reincarnation, an image that is prominent in Buddhism. The various figures and animals in different compartments show that people will either be reincarnated into a higher or lower life depending on their karma. After so many years it is not a surprise that the paint has faded, which helped define the different aspects of the overall piece; one can still see hues of blue, white, green and red. There is a man at the very center of the wheel, whose apparent identity may be a revelation to some. In describing the large carving, Michael D. Gunther of *Art and Archaeology* online says that according to author and professor Angela Howard, who wrote the book *Summit of Treasures*, the figure is Zhao Zhifeng! (Gunther) There are actually many small statues mixed in with the Dazu Rock Carvings that represent those who commissioned or funded the works. Extending out from the center are six white 'beams' which look like ribbons.

In a last look at the Dazu Rock Carvings, the largest statue is the "Parinirvana", also called the "Nirvana of Shakyamuni". The name Shakyamuni also means Buddha. The giant figure is covered from above by a long rock overhang with grass on top of that. Of course, he has the third-eye mark on his forehead. The overall coloring on the statue is orange and blue, though quite faded. The Buddha is 'asleep' lying on his right side, with his head pointing left. This pose can be seen in numerous Buddhist pieces in other locations around the world. However, this particular statue is unique. The rich knowledge resource *Cultural China* online, which covers topics including the arts, history, and literature of China, explains that "Unlike lying Buddha statues elsewhere with whole body carved, this one is carved only half of the body, aiming to indicate Buddha is immeasurable" ("The Quintessence"). With his eyes closed, the Buddha appears to just be asleep, but he is really in the state of Nirvana. As is pointed out by Buddhist monk Tsem Rinpoche of Malaysia, the many carvings at Baoding Shan are instructional. He exclaims, "The sequence of reliefs effectively amounts to a manual on ultimate liberation. Zhao promotes the Mahayana ideal that everyone can be saved through various means" (Rinpoche). In fact, a prominent part of the Baoding Shan scenes are accompanying texts which help in guiding faithful visitors.

Moving west, back to Italy some 250 years after the major work at Dazu was done, a now infamous artist was immersed in Christian theological imagery. Sandro Botticelli was a master of painting in the Early and High Renaissance and focused on people in his works. Living during one of the greatest periods in art history, he was contemporaries with Leonardo da Vinci, Michelangelo, and Raphael. In some paintings, he featured mythological figures such as Venus, Mars, and the Centaur. In many other pieces Botticelli featured Christian icons such as Mary, Saint John the Evangelist, the Magi, and the baby Jesus. In discussing the artist's esteem and popularity during his most popular years, *Artble* online, "the Home of Passionate Art Lovers", points out that the artist was invited by the papacy to produce pieces inside the Sistine Chapel; Artble goes on to say that the "honor of decorating the Chapel was only extended to some of the Renaissance's greatest artists, such as Perugino and Michelangelo" ("Sandro"). Botticelli also did work commissioned by the famous and powerful Medici family. Just as it is today, the wealthy want unique and elaborate works, created by the best artists.

In 1495, fifteen years before his death, Botticelli finished his painting "The Chart of Hell". The theme of the 'burning fires' for the sinful in the afterlife was certainly a 'hot' topic. If one was a Roman Catholic in Italy at the time—which most assuredly were—then the church hammered home the connection between sin and eternal dam-

The Art of Death

nation. The map of Hell that Botticelli created was to illustrate part of Dante's *The Divine Comedy*. The artist's depiction of what the underworld might look like takes the form of a funnel with nine levels. Each level shows people who are there for particular sins, such as murder, blasphemy, or sexual deviance. Botticelli added the figures of Dante and the Roman poet Virgil and showed various instances of them touring Hell. One can see a pile of corpses that the two explorers must pass. Below that are sorry souls who must push boulders around. There are also centaurs shooting arrows into sinners trying to run away. Closer to the bottom of the painting are people who are buried alive with their feet sticking up into the air. In 2001 Botticelli's collection of illustrations for *The Divine Comedy* were featured in an exhibition at the Royal Academy in London. In discussing the featured painting, writer Adrian Searle of *The Guardian* newspaper exclaimed, "How many things can you do to a body, or a soul, before it breaks? Everything, the answer seems to be, again and again" (Searle). There are many people today who probably have the same attitude as Searle, and would not take the depiction too seriously. Of course, there are many fundamentalists who feel that the punishments shown in the painting may not be that far off. Either way, the piece is a searing example of afterlife-themed art in the Renaissance.

Approximately 400 years after "The Chart of Hell", the world had been transformed by the end of the Second Industrial Revolution. In the late 1800s India was a colony, being used to make the British Empire wealthier through trade of goods. Many Indians were starting to question the policies and rule of the British. Although new technologies and manufacturing techniques were introduced to the country, there were many traditional aspects of Indian life which did not change much. Religious themed artwork was always familiar and popular, and in the lead-up to the 20th century many Indian artists created fresh works. Oftentimes their pieces were re-interpretations of known Indian artwork.

One of the major art houses of the last decade of 19th century India was the Chore Bagan Art Studio. It was located in Kolkata—known in English as Calcutta—which is the capital of the Indian state of West Bengal. In his book *Photos of the Gods: The Printed Image and Political Struggle in India*, author Christopher Pinney remarked that the production of prints was a 'vibrant' market by the 1880s. Pinney also points out that "Chore Bagan issued a range of designs paralleling those of the Calcutta Art Studio", which was older and more well-known (27). Many of the pieces that were produced had to do with the afterlife and reincarnation. In 2003 the British Museum in London acquired a Chore Bagan piece from renowned art dealer John Randall, which is entitled "Hell Tortures for Sinners", a part of an album. The museum's curator for the South Asia collection, T. Richard Blurton, comments that most of the prints in this album "reflect Bengal devotional cults" ("2003,1022,0.11"). The featured piece contains eighteen instances of horrible punishments, with the god of death Yama seated in the middle. There are fourteen major panels that line the edges, and five smaller scenes of torture. Yama has an assistant who has the records of each person's life who passes through; there are two men and a woman who are being judged based on their karma, which will be the deciding factor in determining *what* they are in the next life. It may not be surprising that almost all the demons, as well as Yama and his assistant, are predominantly wearing red clothing; the red garments complement the flames and blood appearing all over. The punishments range from attack by snake, being burned alive, getting stabbed, being cut in half, stung by scorpions, and other gruesome scenarios. The inclusion of demons that have horns, with tails on some, is akin to similar Western art. It may be that around the turn of the 20th century, Western and Eastern artists were influencing each other.

7

The Symphony Within

"Music in the soul can be heard by the universe."

- LAO TZU, Founder of Taoism

IT HAS BEEN SAID that music makes the world go round. Being a musician myself, I agree with this mentality. I am a singer; I write my own lyrics, as well as play guitar and electric bass. Up until ninth grade, I didn't get why most of my fellow students were so enamored with popular music. I didn't really connect with the majority of tunes on the radio, which is probably why today I think that the 90s was the worst decade for music. Or maybe it actually was. Of course, everybody has their own taste in what they listen to; one finds what resonates with them, and makes them feel good.

When the subject of music is brought up, it is usually of the secular type. But what about the sounds that move those within the world of religion? Most who live in America would be familiar with hymns in Christian churches. Those found in the Middle East could identify with a morning chant over loudspeakers, reminding them of the first prayer time of the day. All of the world's major religions today incorporate some kind of music or sound within their normal practices. The late Pope John Paul II once said, "As a manifestation of the human spirit, music performs a function which is noble, unique, and irreplaceable. When it is truly beautiful and inspired, it speaks to us more than all the other arts of goodness, virtue, peace, of matters holy and divine" ("Twenty-four Questions"). Music, which is said to be "divinely-inspired," often assists followers of various faiths to connect in a deeply emotional way to their beliefs.

There are many who probably feel the same way as the Pope did about the effect of music on the psyche of humanity. However, there are some who think that when people feel a moving of "the inward self", it has nothing to do with the divine. One of these individuals is novelist Michael Graziano, Professor of Neuroscience at Princeton University. He is also a self-proclaimed atheist who tries to have an understanding of religion. He says that personally, he feels moved by classical music, but that it simply has to do with the workings of the brain. Graziano hypothesizes that when people are listening to a song that connects with them, that the human brain creates a "state of mind", and that the music track has its own "persona". In this process, the mind's emotional side becomes "invested" in the piece. He equates this sense with how people meld their religion in the world (Graziano).

One man whose viewpoint contradicts Graziano's is the famous Estonian composer Arvo Pärt, who belongs to the Eastern Orthodox Christian religion. He is recognized as one of the top contemporary composers of classical pieces, and has received many honors and awards over the years, since his start in the 1960s. The composer is not trying in particular to write overly religious music, but he wants his music to be able to connect with all people. But he has said that religion does play some part in the creation of his work. According to the New York Times, Pärt's 1984 album "Tabula Rasa" had an "abstract spirituality" which won him a place in the ears of listeners from various faiths. Of his 2009 work "Adam's Lament", whose words are from a monk, Pärt says he intends the name Adam to be a "collective term which comprises humankind in its entirety" (Robin). Much of the composer's music utilizes prayers and human dramas which often have a source in his faith, but like many classical pieces, they are not sung in English. Regardless, it seems clear that masterpieces he has produced over the decades have won hearts and minds all over the world; for some, it is a "soulful" experience.

Gregorian Chant

One of the most identifiable forms of religious chanting today is Gregorian, of the Roman Catholic Church. The name comes from association with Pope Saint Gregory I (590-604), who had been credited with playing a role in creating the framework for the style. However, in a lecture about Catholic chants, Yale Professor Craig Wright says that in fact Gregorian chant "had almost nothing to do with Gregory", and that it began, in some sense, almost half a millennia earlier (Wright).

The words, sung by nuns and monks around the world, are in the Latin form. This language has been a favorite of the Catholic Church over the centuries. There are basic patterns of psalms and prayers that provide the structure of the chants. Normally there are is a small block of sentences, such as three, that are followed by another equal set; this is often seen in secular poetry as well. The musical part of the chanting is shown using neumes, which are groups of notes corresponding to words, and this is laid out on a four bar staff. The note designations, and all of the 'neumatic elements', look very familiar; they are actually the source of current-day sheet music. Oftentimes, a chant will be repeated for particular masses or events. In other circumstances, the chant will be a completely different choice; for a special time of the year for instance.

The music that is Gregorian chant travels beyond the walls of cathedrals and monasteries. Since the advent of music CDs, those with a need for 'healing sounds' have sought out chant recordings from around the globe. Of course, nowadays many people find these albums in digital music stores. As writer Judy Keane of the *Catholic Exchange* online points out, the popularity of Gregorian chant hit a high point with the 1994 release of *Chant* by Spanish Benedictine Monks, which rose to the number three spot on the Billboard 200 chart. Referring to the music as being of 'paradise', Keane argues that it offers people something that popular music like rock or rap cannot, because Gregorian chant "transports us to the spiritual" (Keane).

Native American Chant

Most people have probably heard some form of chanting by Native Americans in TV programs or movies. The music has been an integral part of the native communities for thousands of years, and is often accompanied by dance and drumbeat. In fact, the use of drums plays a key role in the chanting process, which is used to help connect the chanter's spirit to the 'other' side. The various tribes all feel a deep connection with the Earth itself, nature, animals, and the spirit world. Shamans, who are the medicine men/women, use chants to go into trances to seek help from spirits to heal

The Symphony Within

sick tribespeople. According to *The Joy of Sects* website about Native American spirituality, the shamans often utilize trance states through chanting to "learn what they need to know to help heal the body, mind, or soul of a patient" (Occhiogrosso). Of course, in modern Native American society, there are the additional prescription drugs and available hospitals. On the other hand, for many reservations the distance to a doctor or hospital can be quite far. Today, but even more-so in the past, the tribe's shaman has played an important role in the well-being of the whole tribe.

For Native Americans, one of the most important leaders for them is Geronimo, who was an Apache warrior and tribal chief. He was a pivotal figure in the fight against the U.S. government in the mid to late 1800s. Even though he was known for his fighting skills, those who followed him also saw him as a healer. When he would lead men to battle, they would often become injured and need to be treated later on. In other instances the patient was simply sick and would be treated with an herbal remedy. In one case, according to observer stories, Geronimo held a healing ceremony for a man who was bitten by a coyote. During the four night ceremony he prayed and chanted, among other things; the chanting was repeated nightly. The shaman chief, through prayers, understood the nature of the coyote and could see things through its perspective. Geronimo "sang and beat a drum with a curved stick" (Sweeney). He had some songs and chants that he wrote himself. The following lyrics are from the self-titled "Geronimo's Song":

> The song that I will sing is an old song, so old that none knows who made it. It has been handed down through generations and was taught to me when I was but a little lad. It is now my own song. It belongs to me. This is a holy song (medicine-song), and great is its power. The song tells how, as

> I sing, I go through the air to a holy place where Yusun (The Supreme Being) will give me power to do wonderful things. I am surrounded by little clouds, and as I go through the air I change, becoming spirit only. ("Geronimo")

Vedic Chant

The Indian Vedas are a large collection of ancient sacred texts that date back more than 3,000 years. They are the oldest Hindu scriptures, and are divided into four parts: the Rigveda, Yajurveda, Samaveda, and Atharvaveda. There has been a long-standing tradition of teachers passing on the Vedas to their students through chanting; various methods have been established by different schools to help students understand and recite verses. Oral memorization has successfully passed the Vedas along from one generation to the next. First announced in 2003, UNESCO (United Nations Educational, Scientific and Cultural Organization) officially added Vedic Chanting to its Representative List of the Intangible Cultural Heritage of Humanity in 2008. Since its start in 2003, the list has encompassed many valued traditions from countries all over the planet. In the context of an ever-changing world, UNESCO explains that "While fragile, intangible cultural heritage is an important factor in maintaining cultural diversity in the face of growing globalization" ("What is"). According to the organization, the number of Indian Vedic recitation schools used to be 1,000, but there are now only thirteen still active.

When chanting Vedic mantras (sacred utterances), one must have strong faith and willpower, according to Gyan Rajhans. A Canadian, originally from India, Mr. Rajhans "has been broadcasting the only non-commercial Vedic re-

The Symphony Within

ligion radio program in North America since 1981 and a global web cast on bhajanawali.com since 1999" (Das). He believes chanting mantras can help to bring one to a higher-self; this means that a chanter could attain a greater level of consciousness. He says that the sounds produced while chanting can affect one's subconscious, in a similar way to how natural sounds influence people, such as wind or thunder.

Rajhans points out that normally the chanting starts and ends with vocalizing 'Om', which is essentially the shortest mantra. He explains that Hindus surmise that Om came into being with the genesis of the Universe itself. Surprisingly, he says that some contemporary philosophers who focus on Vedic thought have found an agreeable passage in the Christian Bible, related to Om. Rajhans looks at the Bible verse, "In the beginning was the Word and the Word was with God and the Word was God" (John 1:1) and asserts that these philosophers associate Om directly with God. In fact, he says that some researchers of Transcendental Meditation believe that chanting Om and other mantras can, through a combination of science and spirituality, heal people.

According to Rajhans, potential healing from chants will be more effective when coming from a 'guru'. This would be a spiritual teacher. He says that he was taught a specific mantra to chant by his personal Guru. He has been chanting it for more than a few decades now, and claims that it has helped keep evil at bay, as well as given him success in life. Rajhans has included the chanting at important junctures of his life, such as "beginning a journey, a new job, or before entering into any new contract or business" (Rajhans). He is truly thankful to his Guru for teaching him the particular mantra. With a focused mind, as well clear goals, he says that chanting mantras is beneficial both bodily and spiritually.

Jewish Cantillation

The practice of Jewish chanting is also known as cantillation, which roughly means 'to sing'. Contextually, the focus for followers is on the Torah, Talmud, and other scriptures. The Torah is the key component of Jewish holy texts and is known as the five books of Moses. The Talmud is basically a collection of additional writings by Rabbis over the centuries, which provide historical commentary on the scriptures. The entire Jewish Bible is called the Tanakh, and also includes books that are found in the various Christian bibles.

To trace where chanting began in Judaism, one must go back thousands of years. The Jewish leader and scribe Ezra is credited with vocalizing the sacred texts to large groups of Jews a half century before the AD era. Ezra's method of communicating the readings with a focus on pitch and rhythm was more than just speaking, but not quite singing either (Edelman). Over the next 1,500 years, various Jewish leaders pronounced the value of chanting the scriptures and the tradition became more defined. It was around 900 AD when instructional notations were added to the sacred texts for use in chanting. A group of scribes known as the Masoretes took it upon themselves to come up with standardized vowel and cantillation markings. Today, the printed Torah "known as *Chumashim*, commonly contain not only the vowel markings, but also cantillation marks" (Davidson).

The markings that indicate how to chant the sacred texts are often referred to as 'tropes'. These are found above and below, as well as inside the words. Tropes assist readers in bringing the text into a musical dimension. According to *LearnTrope* online, which provides lessons for chanting the Torah, "The melody of the verses elevates the spiritual effect on those listening to it and helps to distinguish that text as something holy" (Katz). As is evidenced in traditions all over the world, chanting of religious texts is a common human bond, which brings a 'oneness' between followers and scriptures. In Judaism, instruction in cantillation begins at a young age and is a valuable aspect of the faith.

In the Spring of 2013, Johanna Ginsberg, a writer for *New Jersey Jewish News*, was able to get insights from Jewish chanting expert Rabbi Shefa Gold. Gold originally became interested in Jewish cantillation years earlier, after talking with Rabbi Lawrence Kushner, who promotes some of the mystical aspects of the Jewish faith. Ginsberg, in an article, described a workshop that Gold held in New Jersey, which saw over 50 people in attendance. The event was visited by Jews from local liberal branches. The Rabbi, in her book *The Magic of Hebrew Chant*, exclaimed that she is "drawn toward simplicity in my spiritual practice" (Ginsberg). Gold said that while going through rabbinical school, she was overwhelmed by the great number of scriptures, ciphers, commentaries, and even opinions on the latter. Over the years, she has worked to teach Jewish chanting in a simpler way than is conservatively learned. The Rabbi seems to think that chanters in a group should be less focused on their own self and more on a spiritual harmony. She sees the result of chanting as a 'healing of the spirit'.

Qur'an Reading

Starting in 610 AD, the prophet Muhammad reported that he starting receiving divine revelations, which were verses. He would write down these revelations over a few decades and after his death they were compiled into what became the Qur'an, which is the Muslim holy book. Followers of Islam believe that the holy text is the very word of God and that all actions in life can be guided by it. There are 114 chapters in the Qur'an, which explain how Allah wants his followers to act in life. Muslims utilize their holy book in their five required prayers each day.

One of the main aspects of worship in Islamic mosques is Qur'anic chanting. According to Oxford Islamic Studies Online, "The *Quran* is the focus of rhythmic chanting and the art of calligraphy—the most highly developed artistic skills in Islamic culture" ("Quran"). In the Middle East, as well as other places, the sound of the chants can be heard through mosque loudspeakers. In the early days of the religion, the predominant way of learning the Qur'an was for devotees to simply hear it being spoken to them by an Imam (leader). Starting back then, and continued today, followers would recite verses by repeating them aloud. Over the years a number of ways were developed for chanting the Qur'an. As is pointed out on *IslamiCity* online, a resource which "provides a non-sectarian, comprehensive and holistic view of Islam and Muslims to a global audience", the different chanting traditions "carefully preserved the elaborate science of reciting the Quran – with all its intonations and its cadence and punctuation" ("Islam").

In the article "The Holy Qur'an And The 'Psyche'" written by Mustafa Mahmood, on *Islamic Writings* online, he alludes to there being a transformational aspect on souls through the Qur'an. He says the holy scriptures describe there being a total of seven conditions of the human soul; this means a movement from negative aspects to a balancing and finally a pure state. Mahmood explains that one can go from one level "to the next, higher and higher still, through obedience to Allah and genuine worship" (Mahmood). Certainly the practice of Qur'anic chanting, which has a musical feel, is a main component in worshipping Allah. The most extensive album set ever recorded of Islamic chanting, that is available to the western world, is *The Music of Islam* series. A collection of seventeen CDs, the recorded material equals around twenty hours, and was sourced from nine countries ("The Music"). The producers of the music note that there are variations among the countries in terms of pronunciation and inflection. They also say that the sounds of the chanting may be 'striking' to westerners. However, even though there is an association with music, the producers point out that listeners are really hearing prayers; there were specifically two major prayer types covered, which were the 'ezan' and 'tekbir'. The album producers explain that the prayer, "like the chanting of the Buddhist monks of Tibet, has as its ultimate aim not a musical goal but a spiritual one" ("The Music of Islam,").

Buddhist Chant

There are two major branches of the Buddhist religion: Theravāda and Mahayana. Devotees follow the teachings of Siddhartha Gautama, the Buddha, who lived around the 5th century BC. The name Buddha means "the awakened one". Both branches have traditions of chanting scriptures from the Dharma, which are the official teachings that have been passed down. According to Rev. Jandure Pagngnananda, a Sri Lankan Buddhist monk who runs *Buddhist Page* online, the purpose of religious chanting can vary based on the faith; he says that Theravāda Buddhism "does not consider chanting to be prayer" (Pagngnananda). He explains that chanting improves followers' fervor for the faith and that improves the energy within.

There are a number of official texts which are used in the chanting process. Some see more use depending on the branch involved. Buddhists chant from what are called 'sutras', which are lessons taught by the Buddha or his direct pupils. Many sutras found in Mahayana Buddhism came into being after the Buddha's passing. Sometimes chanting is focused on only a handful of words, while in other situations entire passages are used. Adherents believe that continuous chants can help the inner self and can even have a healing potential. It is said that thoughtful chanting moves followers one step closer towards enlightenment. As Barbara O'Brien, a Zen Buddhist and *About.com* Buddhism writer, points out, "Enlightenment (bodhi) is awakening from one's delusions, especially the delusions of the ego and of a separate self" ("Chanting"). Buddhists see all things as being connected, and that the matter and mental states of people are always in flux.

Oftentimes the practice of reciting Dharma verses is referred to as 'Paritta' chanting, which means 'protection'. Buddhists believe that if one is facing ill health, bodily or mentally, that chanting can effect change in a positive direction. According to *Maithri Publications*, a comprehensive online resource for Theravāda Buddhism, "'Paritta' chanting belongs to the realm of spiritual beauty" ("Buddhist"). Maithri also points out that there will always be doubters in the scientific world of the power of chanting, without physical scientific proof. For devotees of Buddhism, all they need is faith.

Chanting also has its place in the transition into the afterlife. Within Mahayana Buddhism there are followers who belong to what is called the "Pure Land School", which saw its start in China. They believe that with the right steps in life, upon death, one can be reborn into what Buddha called the 'Pure Land'. In discussing the rebirth process, the *Buddha Sutras Mantras Sanskrit* informational website says that the majority of Buddhist temples in China offer a care service for the dying; this consists of a group called Lotus Friends, who not only assist in one's physical needs, but provide chanting of the 'Amitābha Buddha' during the death process. The chants take place before, during, and after death. For those watching over the one who is a 'passing consciousness', they "serve to bear witness to favorable signs, if any, of rebirth in the Pure Land" (Rulu). The chanters cannot know if the person went to the Pure Land, or if they had a different destiny, but they can recall if the individual reported visions of the intended destination.

8

A Force Unleashed

"As long as I can remember I feel I have had this great creative
and spiritual force within me that is greater than faith,
greater than ambition, greater than confidence,
greater than determination, greater than vision.
It is all these combined. My brain becomes
magnetized with this dominating force
which I hold in my hand."[14]

- BRUCE LEE

ALL ACROSS the globe there are those who choose to better themselves by pushing their mind and body further than the day before. Whether it's for exercise, learning defensive moves, or spiritual/personal growth, the martial arts have been a vehicle for these for thousands of years. Individuals who join a particular style must have focus and discipline. Students also learn to re-

---

[14] "Bruce Lee" (See Bibliography)

spect others and most importantly the instructor. While observers see martial artists in a physical fashion, for the students there is also a deeper change within.

A great unifier of traditional martial arts, such as Kung Fu and Tai Chi, is the belief in an inner energy within all of us, which the Chinese call 'chi' and the Japanese pronounce as 'ki'. These essentially translate as 'life force'. Chi is also found in all other living beings, and throughout the Universe. Practitioners of Tai Chi, perhaps the most graceful martial art form, must have an understanding of the 'Yin-Yang'. The symbol for this concept, well-known even in Western countries, is two equal parts within a circle. One side is black and the other is white, with the two halves resembling reversed commas. Within each is a dot with the opposite color within it. The two apparently opposite parts are really reciprocal. The Yin can be thought of as darkness or rest and the Yang as light or activity. As writer Robert Buratti explains in his insightful article "The Spiritual Dimensions of the Martial Arts" in *New Dawn Magazine*, "Without this spiritual dimension to the art, the student is not practicing Tai Chi, they are simply performing empty movements of little significance to themselves or the world around them" (Buratti). In fact, this type of situation is sometimes a concern with martial arts studios in Western nations like the United States. Of course, in many of these countries the prevailing religion is not an Asian one. For an instructor, their program may be a delicate balance of class time, age range of students, as well as social and demographic considerations.

One of the most influential martial arts to be born out of the 20th century is Aikido. It was started in Japan before WWII by Morihei Ueshiba, who is often referred to by students as 'O'Sensei', which means 'Great Teacher'. This particular style is centered on defense and graceful deflection of attacks. One of Ueshiba's direct 'disciples', and first foreign

A Force Unleashed

student, the late French-born master André Nocquet once said that "The practice of Aikido allows the reconciliation between body and spirit" (Nocquet). He saw the two moving together harmoniously. There are a small number of surviving black & white film clips which show Ueshiba practicing moves with his students. The smoothness with which the master 'throws' the students by redirecting their own energy momentum—a melding with the 'attacker's' movement—is astounding. He, an old man, would fend off men in their twenties with little effort. Aikido's founder, among many teachings, said that "To injure an opponent is to injure yourself. To control aggression without inflicting injury is the Art of Peace" ("Morihei"). He believed that all people, including their collective spiritual energy, come from the same place and are all innately connected.

In his master's thesis submitted to the Department of Comparative Religion at Western Michigan University, entitled "Aikido as Spiritual Practice in the United States", Japanese martial arts practitioner Peter Boylan conducted interviews with thirty-three American Aikido adherents; they had been practicing Aikido between one and a half to twenty-three years. Boylan's original hypothesis was, as he put it, that "for many Aikido practitioners, Aikido serves as a portion of their active religious practice" (Boylan). In some of Morihei Ueshiba's teachings, he stressed how Aikido connected with the divine. In fact, he once remarked, "The great spirit of Aiki enjoins all that is divine and enlightened in every land. Unite yourself to the Divine, and you will be able to perceive God wherever you are" ("O'Sensei"). When Boylan talked with the various dojo (school) members, he found that the majority of them came from Catholic backgrounds. On the other hand, many of the interviewees did not belong to a religious group with strict interpretations. A number of them had mixed Aikido in with other 'philosophies' to piece together their own personal religious viewpoint. Around half of the group were confident that 'O'Sensei' was divinely-inspired and had abilities beyond that of the normal human being. Ueshiba himself said that his martial art form came through him from the kami, or 'Divine'. Boylan points out that practitioners can think of kami as 'God', but can refer to their recognized names for the supreme being. He concluded that for two-thirds of the Aikido followers he spoke with, the spiritual component was integral.

Interview with the Lees

In 2010, I was living with two other young guys and my cat in my second apartment, which was basic but decent. We stuck out like a sore thumb, as every other renter was a family. Even still, we tried to be responsible, pay the rent on time (usually), and be respectful of the landlord and neighbors. I had left my first college five years before, and that winter I had a full-time job in the car rental industry. Even though I only had to pay a third of the rent, money was still fairly tight. I enjoyed living on my own, and played rock music in a local band. Overall, things were going pretty well. I enjoyed coming home from work to my own place, kicking back and playing video games. But something was missing. I wanted to push myself farther, and I decided that the martial arts might be the answer. I was looking to improve myself physically, as well who I was on the inside. I had seen some martial arts schools in my city, but I was more familiar with a city I had previously lived in, which was Manchester, the largest city in the state of New Hampshire. After seeing various listings for schools, I decided to observe a lesson at a place called Lee's Martial Arts. All I knew was that the Korean martial art of Tae Kwon Do was taught there. I had planned on visiting additional schools which taught various

A Force Unleashed

disciplines. However, after watching the lesson at this first stop, I was sold. I had worried that some of the newer schools in the area might provide an inauthentic experience, but I could tell that here that wasn't the case. This began my year of discovery.

In January 2015, I went back to visit where my introduction to the martial arts happened. Lee's Martial Arts was founded in 1979 in Manchester, N.H. Today, founder Grand Master Jong Soo Lee still runs the school with his wife Master Linda Lee. In addition to their teaching, there are nine other instructors, who range from 4th to 7th Dan (degree) Black Belts. Included in this group is Master Jong Nam Lee, Jong Soo's brother, a 7th Dan Black Belt. Linda holds a 5th Dan Black Belt. Together, they teach people of all ages, but mostly younger students. For the Lees, it is the quality of instruction that makes their school stand out above the rest.

The Grand Master immigrated to the United States in the 1970s, with a dream to start a new life and bring his expertise in Tae Kwon Do to America. Before this, he graduated from DK University Physical Education Department in Korea. After years of learning the way of Korea's martial art, he began to share his knowledge of TKD. He was part of the Tae Kwon Do Association Demonstration Team, was a National Tournament Referee, and even started an early school in Korea. Once he was in the US, in addition to starting Lee's Martial Arts, he was also the Head Instructor for TKD clubs at Plymouth State University and Dartmouth College in New Hampshire. He attained his final Dan in 2005. Today, at 64, the Grand Master is a 9th degree Black Belt, the highest rank in the World in TKD. He is one of the most senior instructors in the country.

According to Kukkiwon, the World Taekwondo Headquarters in South Korea, there are inevitably different types of instructors. There are the ones who are oppressive, the ones who are too permissive of mistakes and bad attitudes,

A Spirit In Motion

and the type who are fair, keep good morale and teach consistent technique. When I asked the Grand Master about his early training in his homeland, I was surprised at his response. He said that his first instructor was abusive and used his students for his own gains. He moved on, finding more appropriate masters from whom he could learn the true spirit of TKD. As Kukkiwon states in their official textbook, a good instructor must work towards positive & rational thinking, as well as being a model of moral values. The master must be able to help bring out the inner potential of his or her students. Reflecting on his experience with his first instructor, as well as his own desire to teach, the Grand Master explains, "I wanted to teach the right Tae Kwon Do technique and philosophy" (Lee).

As the Lees stress, Tae Kwon Do—as well as other martial arts—should really be approached like an apprenticeship. It is an endeavor which takes years of commitment. As Master Linda told me, "In the oriental philosophy, when you get your first black belt, you've just started your journey." But even the white belt student knows that each person in the dojang is practicing a particular set of movements, called 'poomsae' (forms). There are eight poomsae leading up to black belt, which are collectively called 'Taegeuk'. These correspond to the level of the student. I am a green belt, which means the last form I trained in was 'Taeguek Sam Jang', which means the student has energetic passion in continued learning. There are nine poomsae for black belts. It is important to keep in mind that the moves which comprise these forms have progressed to modern day after centuries of Korean martial arts. Some of the symbolism of TKD forms originates from Taoism. The first black belt form is 'Koryo', for the one who has a "righteous learned spirit". Over the years, trained students become instructors and masters, up to the final poomsae; the last form is called 'Ilyeo'. This is the crowning line of movements, perfected

A Force Unleashed

only by grand masters. In explaining the background of Ilyeo, Kukkiwon says that it represents the third king of the renowned Korean Buddhist priest Wonhyo, who lived during the Silla Dynasty in the 7th century. The concept is the union of body and spirit. Kukkiwon says that in the final sequence of this training, "two wrapped-up fists are placed in front of the chin, which has the significance of unification and moderation, so that the spiritual energy can flow freely into the body as well as the two hands." This final form is a symbol of the many years of cultivation of technique, spirit and body in TKD. It shows a true harmony. Of course, this doesn't mean that a grand master only has to focus on this final form. Master Linda told me that doing the same forms (all nine), later, as a teacher, is different, because you see things better and can do better.

I asked the Grand Master whether TKD and students are different now than in the past. He reveals that courtesy, discipline, perseverance, and an endurable spirit are lacking in each new generation as people are changing. He has been involved with TKD since childhood and has seen it spread from Korea to places like the U.S. He believes that "Everything's changing in the martial arts." He has noticed that, generally, students' focus of energy and concentration is different now than it used to be. Reflecting back on the early days of Lee's Martial Arts, from the late 70s to the late 80s, the Grand Master's original students—mostly adults—were driven and had focus. In the 80s and 90s, the Lees went to many tournaments with their best students. In recent years, society has changed and students are typically younger these days. The lives of both students and their families move at a faster pace. The minds of kids and teens face ever-growing distractions in an American society—as well as others—which seems to sometimes offer decreasing guidance on the path of life. The Grand Master reveals, "I'm worried what will happen in fifty years." The instructors want students to be able to realize an inner balance through TKD; this not only takes great leadership on the part of the masters, but also a willingness by students to grow. Some students go the extra measure and display a drive from within. The Lees told me that, perhaps, five percent of students could be labeled as exceptional. Yet, it is hard to single out a certain student–in a class of many–who excels, in order to get him or her on to the next point in their training. There is also the occasional student who is problematic, which tends to be found with the younger students. Master Linda believes that "Kids need character building. They're victims of themselves." The Grand Master can sense bad apples and sometimes kicks them out of the dojang. The philosophy and teaching are most important, and there is no time for students like that. Such students can cause others to lose mental focus. Even though, as the Grand Master points out, there is different thinking and philosophies between the various martial arts, the Lees referenced the now iconic teacher–played by the late Noriyuki "Pat" Morita–in *The Karate Kid*. Master Linda says, "We can relate to Mr. Miyagi. Don't question the master, trust him." From my own personal experience in the Lee's dojang, I can attest to this being a key aspect of training in TKD. The martial arts master will reveal more than flying fists and feet. It is the unseen part of training which will test the inner spirit and perseverance of students, especially in adults.

Lee's Martial Arts operates in a fairly diverse city, where people from different countries, religions, and world-views live together. In the Grand Master's birthplace of Korea, the spiritual beliefs and background of the people are very similar. America, in contrast, holds much more variation in these things. The Grand Master feels that there does not need to be a direct connection between religion and today's TKD. He related to me that in modern Korea, the spiritual aspect is not really involved much with the country's signature martial art. I asked him about the term "Seon" and it's relation to TKD. It is a basic meditation practiced in some Korean and international dojang, in which students sit still quietly. He recalls that when he was just starting out in the martial art in Korea, Seon was practiced in the dojang for a few minutes at the end of class. This practice is not included in this way in his American TKD school. The Grand Master explains, "I want to teach traditional Tae Kwon Do, but I have included less and less of the spiritual and philosophy, because it's not politically correct anymore." The Lees instruct their students in the most genuine way possible, but have also adapted their instruction of TKD for a changing American demographic. The majority of what many would term as "intense" TKD dojang are located in the largest cities in the U.S. and mostly deal with adult students. The Lee's goal is to develop their wide-ranging students with a focus on strength in heart, spirit, and body. The Grand Master says, "Improving the mind and body is very important in the martial arts." Master Linda adds, "Tae Kwon Do is working to better yourself. It is a way of life." She also thinks that taking TKD allows adults a sense of being and leadership, and to go out into the world with confidence. Coming from a female perspective, in a sometimes male-heavy martial arts world, she adds, "Learning to deal with the outside world, women must have confidence and go with their inner instinct. This is so important. Being able to deal with different personalities and understanding others is an important part of TKD." Regardless of gender or background, students should realize the importance of "jung shin yuk" in TKD, which is mental power. The Grand Master also describes the meaning for students as "don't give up". In order for students to be serious practitioners, they must break the barriers in their mind, which hold them back from realizing their inner potential.

The Grand Master told me that, once and a while, a student will train under him after coming from another school and will bring with them external practices. He recalls a transfer student, who once attended, who drew the attention of the Grand Master and the other students; the student, who had to start afresh with a white belt, was holding the belt–before entering the practice area–up in the air in front of his chest. The Grand Master asked him what he was doing. It was some kind of ceremonial move which had spiritual connotations. He told the student that that practice wasn't done in his dojang. As mentioned, due to changing times and generational culture, the Grand Master has left out the more intricate philosophies and spiritual ideals attached to the TKD of Korea's past. He concludes that "generations are changing and they don't want to go that deep." To illustrate this, he gives the analogy of an apple; the outside is there for all to see, but it is only the beginning. The deeper meaning of their journey in Tae Kwon Do lies inside, beyond the skin. The Grand Master reveals that the skin is tasty, but most students won't attempt to go to the core. He says young adults, today, do not want to cut open the apple to reveal the seeds.

One of the recognized martial artists who was involved in aikido, as well as nine other forms, was Joe Hyams (1923-2008). He worked as a syndicated columnist and author, and was mainly active in the martial arts between the 50s and 70s. He was from Massachusetts, served in WWII, and spent most of his life in California. Due to his press associations and Hollywood connections, and perhaps amazing luck, he knew and trained under some of the great martial art masters. Hyams first teacher was the legendary Ed Parker, who is considered the father of American kenpo-karate. He was one of Parker's early students, and would go on to earn his first black belt under his leadership. In the mid 1960s, shortly after Hyams watched Bruce Lee perform in a tournament, he was able to meet the now legendary icon. Lee did not have his own school yet, but Hyams asked if he could become his private student. Lee accepted and the training continued for a couple years. Lee was teaching his own new form called jeet-kune-do. Hyam's third major instructor was Bong Soo Han, the famous Korean master of hapkido, who began training him in 1973. Han is seen as the father of hapkido in the West.

In 1979, Hyams published *Zen in the Martial Arts*, which went on to be quite successful and well-regarded. Even today, those who read it for the first time almost universally write warm online reviews of the book. It was his reflection on what he had learned from almost twenty-five years in the martial arts and how he had applied that to his personal life. The author was aware of many other books that had been written on the martial arts, but saw that most were focused on the physical movements and little else. When Hyams first started kenpo-karate, he went through the normal motions of a learning student, but as time went on he realized there was more to it than the physical. Eventually, as he reveals in his book, he determined that "the deepest purpose of the martial arts is to serve as a vehicle for personal spiritual development" (10). He discovered Zen, which has its source in Buddhism and is an understanding of oneself while unifying the body and mind. People often say that Zen is a "way of being". Hyams explained Zen's meaning for the martial arts as aiding in removal of "anger, illusion, and false passion". He didn't believe that the average student could realize Zen in the early part of training, but that it takes time. Students must make their best effort, while their master illuminates the path in a spiritual sense, which should, combined, reveal the truth of the martial arts to each student.

Hyams had a passion for learning the way of numerous martial art forms, as well as considering how they affected his 'inner-self'. After having an interest in Aikido for years, he witnessed a demonstration one time in London of that form by a Japanese master. A number of large men surrounded the master and launched a staged attack, so that the utilization of the ki in aikido could be shown to onlookers. The master seemed to effortlessly evade blows and redirect the men coming at him. Hyams recalled thinking that this Japanese man had moved as if he was made up of water. It should not be surprising that Hyams saw it that way, considering that his past teacher Bruce Lee is known for instructing students to "be water". The master, who Hyams doesn't name, also wanted an observer to try to pull him up from where he was standing. Hyams himself got in on the action and volunteered. To his surprise, he could not move the smaller Japanese man. The master told him that it was because of ki. Hyams recalled that there was definitely something invisible and mysterious going on. Later on, when he went to an Aikido school, he was told that the ki is a universal energy that intersects one's body around the bottom of the belly and that one can send that energy towards another point, like the end of an arm. It can even be pushed outside the body towards another person or object.

In a final look at *Zen in the Martial Arts,* Hyams also talked about the well-known concept of "mind over matter". This usually has to do with someone doing something that goes beyond what should normally be possible. He recalled visiting the dojang (training area) of Master Yong Tae Lee in 1975, a 7th degree black belt in tae-kwon-do. The master was readying himself for a match he had to fight in and was punching a piece of wood. Hyams and a friend noticed that the master's knuckles were not looking so good; they were actually bleeding! Lee explained that he could go somewhere else in thought virtually so that he would not feel the pain. He then told the two men a story about his own master in Korea. He said that his master had a major problem with his sinuses and would need surgery, at almost 90 years old. Lee's master told the surgeon that he would undergo the procedure without anesthetic! He was able, under the knife, to free his mind from his body and not sense the pain. This feat, Lee told the men, is combined with a breathing technique, which Hyams links with Zen. He said that he was able to use this valuable lesson in his own life multiple times.

Almost all of the well-known martial arts originate from Asia; this includes forms already mentioned, as well as shaolin kung fu, tai chi, shorinji kempo, and others. With this reality come connections to Buddhism, Taoism, and other philosophies. How far these links are stressed in martial arts schools vary, especially in the US and Europe. Since the increased Western interest in many martial arts around the mid-20th century, some have raised concerns about an Eastern influence on the religion of the majority. The Christian community, largely, views the martial arts as a positive in the community. However, a minority of conservative groups claim that their beliefs conflict spiritually with martial arts that come from the East. Similar arguments surfaced during the counterculture movement of the 1960s, though applied to numerous issues.

One group that holds this view is VMTC International, which stands for Victorious Ministry Through Christ. Founded in 1971, it is an interdenominational organization whose focus is on training members of churches in spiritual healing & growth, and prayer. They operate out of nine countries. In an article on their main website entitled "Exposing Martial Arts", the group's secretary and New Zealand chapter President, Rev. Brian Brandon, claims that Westerners try to separate the spiritual from the martial arts and simply label it as a sport. He explains that this does not work because the original Eastern belief behind it sees the physical and spiritual as being inherently bonded together. Brandon believes that the concept of ki is antithetical to the Christian idea of the spirit and asserts that it is not of God. In fact, he boldly claims that the martial arts "spiritual basis has been largely still hidden, and people are initiated into the practices without being told about the occult basis" (Brandon). He sees martial arts studios marketing and communications efforts towards prospective students being presented in an all-inclusive manner, but that it is a way of sweeping under the rug particular concepts; this includes ideas about spiritual healing. Brandon concludes that those of the Christian faith, especially 'impressionable' youth, should not be involved in the martial arts, because it could harm them spiritually.

The views expressed by organizations like VMTC are certainly *not* mainstream and have been challenged by many; one of these alternate interpretations comes from Master Jeffrey Moore, the National Director of The American Federation of Jujitsu and Director of The International Federation of Yoshin Ryu Jujitsu. He discloses that the AFJ is sometimes contacted by students and parents who have apprehensions about possible allusions to Eastern religion within Jujitsu classes. He says that all people have spirits, which he uses in place of the word 'soul', and that whether we go to an afterlife or not, our spirits are joined with the mental and physical through our earthly lives. Moore argues that spiritual development is important in the martial arts, but that those who see it as religion are "inexperienced". The balancing of mind, body and spirit takes time, and in the beginning the focus is on learning moves which form the basis of a particular martial art. He admits that some masters who own their own schools will involve some religious concepts within the overall teaching; he gives the example of studios that include the word 'Christian' in their name, which he says are an open way of attracting students from that kind of background. Still, that does not mean that someone from another faith absolutely cannot join. In fact, he proclaims that if an instructor is using a martial art to quietly instill specific religious values into their students that were not mentioned in the beginning, then they are doing the wrong thing. Moore believes that in Jujitsu, as well as the other forms, "when the mind, body and spirit unite for just a second or two, the technique will be effortless and perfect" (Moore). For early learners, this is not that common. As students progress and mature, they begin to feel this united technique. As Moore contends, the proper path of students is to first work on the mechanics of the discipline and later on to come to an understanding of integration of the unseen component.

In further contrast to Brandon's (as well as others') claim that Christian spiritual belief cannot mix with the martial arts, there is a force, an icon, who stands in the way. Arguably a legend, as well as a rockstar of the "Christian right", Chuck Norris would appear to break that allegation into pieces. He was most active in the martial arts between the late 50s to early 70s, with a focus on Tang Soo Do and Judo. He fought in numerous karate championships, held the title of World Professional Middleweight Karate Champion for six years, and owned his own chain of karate schools in the 60s. Norris began his film fame when he famously squared off against Bruce Lee in the epic 1972 film *The Way of the Dragon*.[15] After his film career had slowed down, Norris cre-

---

[15] Lee and Norris actually knew each other beforehand, since they met at the 1968 World Professional Karate Championship at Madison Square Garden in NYC. They became friends, often working out together, practicing moves. Lee asked Norris to be in the film. (CNBC)

ated a new martial art called Chun Kuk Do in 1990. In the same year, he became the first Westerner in history to earn an 8th degree black belt in Tae Kwon Do. Since then, he has been a strong supporter of kids becoming involved in the martial arts. In that same time he has been clear in his alignment with the Christian Evangelical movement.

In 1996, Norris published his book *The Secret Power Within: Zen Solutions to Real Problems*. In a look back on his career and personal life, he shares with readers how, like him, they can apply the ancient philosophy of Zen to their own lives. In the book, he talks about links to the martial arts, as well as Zen's applicability to normal situations. He talks about having confidence, aiming for success, and not believing in limits. Norris reminisces about meeting a Buddhist monk in 1962, who would sometimes sit and watch him teach his karate class. The monk, it turned out, was also a martial artist. He came from a local temple. The Buddhist told Norris all about ki, Zen, and the third eye.[16] Even though he had a realization of the martial arts beyond the physical, Norris did not adopt the Buddhist religion, as he says the monk had wished. Norris was already committed to his Christian faith. He did, however, see the importance of keeping an open mind. This would become one of his founding rules of Chun Kuk Do. He also touches on *enlightenment*, but not in the sense which it is normally referred to in Buddhism; he's not talking about the final moment of pure realization of existence in the lifecycle of a Buddhist. Norris lays it out in a simple way. Whether one is in the martial arts dojo, or at work, or walking down the sidewalk, one can have a flash of enlightenment. He believes we must not become stuck in how we see the world and other people.

---

[16] The third eye is a concept found not only in Buddhism, but also Taoism, Hinduism, and other beliefs. It is said to be an invisible eye, possibly related to the pineal gland, which allows one to spiritually see things (normally with the physical eyes closed) beyond what normal sight allows for. This is supposed to be located between one's eyes, but slightly above.

A Force Unleashed

He maintains that when that moment occurs, "nothing changes except our point of view, and that changes everything forever" (Norris). He explains that people need to make that decision to keep moving forward in life, applying Zen as action towards achieving happiness and real understanding of their life. Norris also makes it clear that there is a strong connection between Zen and the martial arts, and the idea of taking action in one's personal life fits right in here as well. He wants readers to know that no matter who they are, celebrity or not, they can use Zen just like he has. He urges people to reflect on how he utilized Zen in his life and then apply it to their own personal path. On Norris' journey he makes it apparent that ideas like Zen and ki, while Eastern in nature, helped a Western Christian man to see fulfillment as a martial artist.

9

The Scientific Method

> "The best scientist is open to
> experience and begins with romance
> – the idea that anything is possible."[17]
>
> - RAY BRADBURY

WHEN IT comes to believing in evidence of souls, ghosts and paranormal activity, there are three groups of people. There are the believers, the ones who don't care or are unsure, and then there are the skeptics. Sometimes you get the ones who say that ghosts aren't real, but at some point they have their own experience and change what their accepted reality is. For those who say there is no possibility of an afterlife or ghosts, there were also people who used to say the world was flat. Many scientists today, it is probably safe to say, do not be-

---

[17] "Ray Bradbury" (See Bibliography)

lieve in ghosts and/or paranormal events. For most scientists to be analytical, they have to use known facts and the laws of physics. For most of them, ideas about the afterlife, poltergeists, ghosts, spirits, or demons, are just too far out there. If they cannot prove the existence of spirits around us by using methods known to them in experiments, or being able to reproduce paranormal traits in the lab, then a lot of them just feel that there is nothing to prove. In more recent times, there are some scientific groups that have put their skepticism to the side, and conducted detailed sessions at locations that are supposedly haunted. Occasionally there are scientists who get involved in these investigations out of curiosity. However, overall, most in the scientific field have *faith* that all things can, in some way, be put to the test by science. For those topics which become encircled by seemingly unending questions, the word 'theory' becomes attached.

Over the years there have been scientists who actually did believe in the afterlife, some of them well known. Take Thomas Edison, for example. He designed the original electrical distribution system in the United States using DC current, although, later on, the AC system that Nikola Tesla designed was incorporated instead by Westinghouse. He also created some of the first incandescent light bulbs used by the public, designed the phonograph, and even worked on developing the motion picture which today we take for granted. There was one concept he had realized though that most people do not know about. Not only did he believe in the afterlife, but that your spirit goes on to somewhere else and can interact with the living. In fact in 1920 he did an interview with the science journal *Scientific American*. Here is a quote from that piece:

> If our personality survives, then it is strictly logical and scientific to assume that it retains memory, intellect and other faculties and knowledge that we acquire on this

The Scientific Method

> Earth. Therefore, if personality exists after what we call death, it is reasonable to conclude that those who leave this Earth would like to communicate with those they have left here… I am inclined to believe that our personality hereafter will be able to affect matter. If this reasoning be correct, then, if we can evolve an instrument so delicate as to be affected or moved or manipulated… by our personality as it survives in the next life, such an instrument, when made available, ought to record something. (Lescarboura)

Well, guess what folks, we do have a number of devices now that are used for that purpose! Edison, just like many great scientists, sometimes came to conclusions that were ahead of his time. Edison was brilliant and his ideas about the afterlife could have some validity. He loved to consider possibilities that didn't exist at the moment, seeming to live for the challenge.

One profession that directly deals with life and death, going beyond scientific theory, is of course medical doctors. They see people brought into the world, and people leaving it behind. They must make their best effort to heal the physical, while often considering the 'inner' person as well. If a patient can be saved, a doctor must do what they can to ensure that result. The majority of med students, upon graduation, will take the Hippocratic Oath. It is a modern version of the original Greek form penned around the 5th century BC.[18] New doctors swear to take great care in life or

---

[18] In the ancient Greek version, it mentioned that the physician swore to the gods and goddesses that they would abide by their oath. It also included an anti-abortion line that said the doctor would not give any medicine to a pregnant woman that would "destroy" the unborn. These things were unsurprisingly taken out of the 20th century rewrites.

death scenarios, understand that illness affects a patient's family, recognize their special responsibility toward other human beings in society, and not assume the role of God.

In the medical field of today, there is a largely unanswered mystery, one that arises during controlled drug trials. Oftentimes, a doctor will issue an experimental drug to a group of volunteers and study what the effect is, but at the same time they give others a placebo. One would think that this latter group would exhibit no recorded bodily changes. However, this is not always the case. This is generally referred to as the "placebo effect". People who unknowingly receive the fake drug usually expect that whatever condition they have will improve. Sometimes, there can actually be recordable changes in the brain. In one study, reported on by Harvard Medical School, placebos were administered to Parkinson's sufferers. These patients' brains do not make enough of the chemical 'dopamine'. Amazingly, the fake medicine helped trigger production of dopamine in the patients ("Putting"). There are many other ailments that are also targeted in these types of drug trials, such as joint pain or depression. Oftentimes, people who are given the faux drug and rise above the sickness are simply released from the study. As was pointed out in a *NY Times* article on the effect, the numbers may become clearer, but "this does not help researchers understand why people in the first group got better" (Vance). Some medical professionals are somewhat dismissive of the results of some of these studies, while others see some of the findings rather baffling.

To many medical researchers, the placebo effect seems to be a natural response of some sort. Yet, for others, there may be more to the story. In fact, in a journal article from the Human Science Center at Ludwig Maximilian University in Germany, it was proposed that there may be a link between the placebo effect and spirituality. Their research supposes that there could be an "eliciting of self-healing processes" if medical professionals, utilizing their knowledge of mind and body, can integrate a patient's own spirituality into treatments (Kohls et al.). They see an apparent connection between spiritual occurrences and improvement of health with placebos, which seems to lie in the mind. Along this same line of thought, journalist and author Richard Schiffman also tackled this subject. He believes that the placebo effect can be associated with prayer and meditation. He feels that it's alright if the field of science can't completely explain what is going on. Schiffman exclaims that it is miraculous that "something immaterial (a thought?) has impacted something material (our body) in a way which utterly defies logic" ("How"). Of course, once the discussion of placebos heads into this kind of territory, some doctors and scientists start to distance themselves. On the other hand, this hasn't stopped some doctors from prescribing placebos to their patients if they believe there will be a positive result.

Interview with Dr. Rick Strassman – Part 2: DMT and the Spiritual Mind

Earlier, in "Forever Faithful: Judaism" (ch. 4), I introduced you to Dr. Strassman; he is Clinical Associate Professor of Psychiatry at the University of New Mexico School of Medicine. In 2000, he published his landmark book *DMT: The Spirit Molecule*. This book details the research study he helmed, starting in 1990, which was the first in over two decades to look at the effects of hallucinogenic/psychedelic drugs–specifically DMT–on the human mind. In 2008, he co-authored *Inner Paths to Outer Space* along with three experts, whose fields cover hematology-oncology, anthropology, psychotherapeutics, psychiatry, phenomenology, and shamanism. The book is meant to be a bridge to the science-fiction community in order to inform them of the DMT research and particularly about study subjects who reported contact with 'beings' while in their psychedelic states. His most recent book is *DMT and the Soul Prophecy: A New Science of Spiritual Revelation in the Hebrew Bible* (2014). Strassman considers some unanswered questions stemming from his groundbreaking research in the early 90s. He also delves into prophetic states found in the Hebrew Bible, as well as the ideas of medieval Jewish philosophers. In discussing the normal scientific reasoning for prophetic states in the mind, he explains that this is "represented by neurotheology wherein changes in brain chemistry give the impression of communicating with the divine, whereas my new model, theoneurology, posits that God communicates with us via the agency of the brain." His research shows a connection between DMT and the pineal gland in the brain, which–as he points out–is believed by Hindus and René Descartes to be where the soul resides.

The fascinating research that Strassman has conducted has taken place over many years and has added greatly to our knowledge of DMT's effects in the human brain. Considering the totality of his published books and the many people who've read them, the impact of the doctor's research delves into spirituality and the possibilities of the mind. I asked Strassman, "What got you interested in the link between DMT, the spirit and the mind?" He recalls, "As an undergraduate I became interested in the biological bases of spiritual experience. The descriptions of the psychedelic drug state and those elicited by certain meditation practices seem to overlap in certain instances to a rather large degree. I thought that there must be some underlying biological phenomenon that might be activated in both syndromes. This got me looking into the pineal gland, as a possible 'spiritual center' in the brain which then led me to learn what the esoteric physiologies of Kabbalah in Hindu-

The Scientific Method

ism—that also believed this to be the case—had to say about it. Thus I was introduced to rather sophisticated notions of the soul and its relationship to the mind and various mental states. After investigating pineal melatonin as a potential mediator of spiritual experiences, and finding that it was relatively inactive, I turned my attention to DMT. This compound had the advantage of being both made in the human body as well as being profoundly psychoactive." The reference to Hinduism is connected to what is called the 'third eye'; this is illustrated by the red dot placed on the center of many Hindu's foreheads. It is a kind of outward visual representation pointing to the area of the brain behind it. It is said that this 'eye' allows one to 'see' more than the straightforward reality apparent to all people.

I noticed the prevalence of Eastern ideas about the connection between the spiritual and the brain in the doctor's writings. He also does comparisons of Western versus Eastern mystical and metaphysical concepts. I asked him, "How have Eastern spiritual beliefs changed the way the West thinks about the inner self, the 'other side', and our understanding of the possibilities of the brain?" Strassman told me that these beliefs, which have migrated to the West, are a "highly sanitized version stripped of the theological and superstitious accompaniments that characterize these religions in their native state." Religions like Buddhism, as I have found in my own research, are quite complicated and can be difficult to translate into the Western way of thinking. The world of spirits and demigods in Buddhism is quite diverse and requires a lot of time to fully understand. As the doctor puts it, "The westernized version of Buddhism has treated all of these phenomena as psychological constructs, something much more palatable to the 'scientific' 'modern' Western mind." He continues, "I think Buddhist psychology has allowed us to view the mind in a novel manner but that Buddhist theology must be understood as the fount out of which Buddhist psychology emerged. Buddhism has particular beliefs about man and his mind, his relationship to the universe both physical and invisible, the ideal way to live and believe, particular notions of life and death, history, and so on. For example, one of the occupations discouraged by Buddhism is medicine, in contrast with, say, Jewish beliefs in the value of that occupation. These different approaches to the practice of, in this case medicine, reflect highly divergent views about mankind and one's relationship with it." Strassman tells me that there seems to be a distorted view of Buddhist ideas, exhibited by some Western enthusiasts, which promulgates the idea that everything we see around us is somehow directly real due to our own conscious existence. He believes that this is no more likely than the opposite view that anything we discern, apart from ourselves, actually does exist around us. In connecting this concept to his lab research, he tells me that "in the spiritual realms, one of the issues I needed to address in my DMT work was the unshakable conviction on the part of my volunteers that the DMT world was not a mental fiction, created by the drug, but an absolutely objective, external, freestanding reality." When someone is used to living their normal day-to-day life, they become used to what is considered reality. They go to work, go food shopping, watch the sun rise and fall in the sky; these events, as well as others, appear to be part of a straightforward world. However, psychedelic compounds like DMT, through effects on the brain, expand a user's worldview. It is, in some sense, a new frontier.

It is hard to argue with a test subject's own DMT-activated experience, in which they are sure of what they sensed and how they interpreted it. As the doctor mentioned, the opinions of his study subjects on whether they had accessed an outside reality—which actually exists—were surely in endorsement of that being truth. This did not seem to match up with his understanding, going into the

The Scientific Method

study, of the belief that alternate realities were a generation of a subject's own mind. Viewing psychedelic states through the lens of Buddhism, Strassman points out the "enlightenment state as the highest possible goal, the gold standard, of spiritual experience, something that has infiltrated the psychedelic drug research arena as well as non-research use, either hedonic or therapeutic. In other words, the goal of spirituality, drug induced or otherwise, within the 'field' and within the academic setting, is that of a unitive enlightenment state. This state consists of the absolute identification with the Buddhist concept of emptiness, a nonverbal, content-free, blissful, unitive state in which the constraints of self, time, and space no longer apply." He says, now comparing this view to Western thought, that "This has had the effect of relegating the paradigmatic Biblical religious experience, prophecy, to the sidelines. This, despite one-half of the world's population practicing a Tanakh-based religion, and the Hebrew Bible's enduring pervasive influence on our civilization: law, theology, art, philosophy, psychology, ethics, economics, wisdom, and so on. Prophecy, like the DMT state, is full of content, experienced and witnessed by a highly maintained sense of self, communicating and interacting with all manner of spiritual beings in a more or less linear temporal manner. The prophetic state, in contrast to the DMT one, however, is highly verbal, and it is the nature of the verbal information that has most likely led moderns to avoid the prophetic state as the goal of spiritual practice in favor of the nonverbal enlightenment one." Of course, Westerner's religious beliefs greatly vary and there are certainly many followers of Abrahamic religions who still value a more traditional view of spiritual experiences. For those who are familiar with psychedelic research, they are likely aware of the plant-based psychedelic experiences found in places like Peru. The doctor tells me, "While the Latin American shamanic movement, especially that promulgating the use of ayahuasca, acknowledges and works with the content-full spiritual worlds revealed through orally active DMT, this is essentially a non-Western, polytheistic, ethically and morally challenged system which has limited applicability to the larger Western culture. The Hebrew Bible's prophetic model, on the other hand, is much more capable of widespread acceptance in the larger traditional Western community, but its moral, ethical, and theological notions are problematic for a liberal, secular, educated population, in particular, those who partake of or study academically the psychedelic drug state. Thus, the more widespread acceptance of the popularized Buddhist 'all is one' morally relative stance to the altered states of the spiritual experience." It may be that for both academic and therapeutic users of psychedelics, there may be a tendency to shelve preconceived religious frameworks of spiritual experiences. Even those, such as DMT test subjects, who hold certain beliefs may have difficulty completely understanding what they sense in alternate states.

Anyone who is familiar with Strassman's work knows that it had, as mentioned earlier, been over twenty years between the previous U.S. government approved psychedelic studies and his. Just to begin DMT testing on volunteer subjects took a lot of patience on the doctor's part and a lot of jumping through hoops. In fact, psychedelic drugs largely became illegal–technically 'schedule-1'–during the conservative administration of Richard Nixon. The use of psychedelics was fairly prevalent in the 1960s, to the dismay of some who thought it was a negative aspect of a growing counterculture. Curious whether this was still a target of critics, I asked the doctor, "How do you view the push-back among Western conservatives against the use of psychedelics?" He responded, "I don't see much pushback. I see the media handling the resurgence in psychedelic drug research with enthusiasm, tact, and balance. I have yet to hear any

The Scientific Method

pushback from conservatives against psychedelic drug research. This is a function of the maturing of the field, its investigators having learned to avoid some of the pitfalls of the earlier generation of scientists, keeping their claims and goals within the scientific paradigm, not using their research as soapboxes upon which to feed their own needs for public adulation, and so on. People will always be 'anti-drug,' but I don't see this taking place in response to bona fide scientific research." Of course, times change and there are always new developments in the word of scientific studies, drug analysis and brain research. There are also many who feel that the U.S. war on drugs—mainly the illicit type—has largely failed, which has led to questions about the use of all types of drugs in society. Today, there are also research studies using psychedelics in applications towards those with terminal illnesses.

Strassman's latest book is an interesting approach to questions of spirituality and the brain, in that it combines his DMT research and prophetic states found in the Hebrew Bible. I asked him, "What are the key takeaways you found in the texts of Jewish philosophers of the past, and how have you brought these ideas into the modern era in your research?" He explains, "They taught me that one could view the Hebrew Bible through the lens of a rational/scientific worldview. That is, one, could be both 'scientific' and 'religious' at the same time—no conflict. Each enhanced the other. The goal of every science in their minds (and probably in the minds of all contemporary scientists) is the ultimate cause and root of their discipline, and this in the medievalists worldview, was God. One learned about God through the study of His creation." Lately, in the U.S., one can certainly come across perceived disagreements within a science versus religion context. Politicians on both sides of the aisle are knocked by the other, as well as in the TV media and social media, about their views on topics like abortion, stem cell research, separation of church and state, and global warming. This brings to mind last year's webcast debate between Bill Nye the Science Guy and Ken Ham, a creationist, who debated "whether creation is a viable model of origins in today's modern scientific era." Nye certainly drew the ire of numerous scientists for even taking part in the debate. Strassman's finding of "no conflict" between being religious and scientific would seem to be beneficial in terms of being open-minded during all stages of his research. In terms of his findings within the Jewish texts, he further explains, "Their metaphysics of the prophetic state provided me with an alternative model for the DMT-induced experience to that of contemporary neurotheology which posits that such experiences are wholly an innate, evolutionarily adaptive reflex of the brain responding to particular stimuli, including drugs, prayer, fasting, and so on. The metaphysics of the medieval Jewish philosophers led me to proposing a theoneurological model in which God has designed the brain in such a way as to allow communication with us. This is a top-down rather than bottom-up model, and is consistent with a theocentric worldview. It doesn't necessarily replace the neurotheological model but provides a counterpoint for one who sees the presence of God in the natural and psychological worlds and is seeking a sophisticated model for how this may happen in the world of spiritual states." This viewpoint can provide a more balanced approach towards understanding the states described by subjects in psychedelic drug studies. Of course, not every person who takes part in being a test subject in a psychedelic drug study is going to share the same background. Thus, they may not interpret their experiences in the same way.

Within this book I have taken a look at the phenomena of out-of-body experiences (OBEs) and near-death experiences (NDEs), in connection with the probable link to the soul. I told the doctor that "The occurrence of OBEs and

The Scientific Method

NDEs raise questions about the nature of consciousness and whether it is a permanent part of the brain." I asked him, "What type of conclusions have you come to about this in your research with DMT?" He told me, "Consciousness is clearly associated with the brain. And changes in brain chemistry are accompanied by changes in consciousness. I've not looked into OBEs in particular, and none of my volunteers went someplace else, such as into another room on the research unit, downtown Albuquerque, etc., so that hasn't been an area I've looked into. I expected more typical NDEs than what occurred in my study as I had hypothesized that DMT might be released when people are dying and that the phenomenology of the two states might overlap. However, in my project only one person had something she referred to as a NDE, and it did share features with the classical reports. But in nearly five dozen subjects, this would qualify as 'quite rare.' Keep in mind that NDEs occur in the 'nearly' dead, not the dead. We don't know what happens after death. There clearly are brain chemistry changes during the dying process, and the residual consciousness that may reside in the brain as we die may perceive some highly altered contents, such as reported in NDEs, the Tibetan Book of the Dead, and so on. But whether this establishes that consciousness, as we normally understand the term, survives after death, is far from certain. The medieval Jewish philosophers suggested that the imagination—where perceptions, emotions, and other 'contents' of the mind reside—is a somatic phenomenon. That would mean that when the body dies, there would be no longer be left any perceptions, emotions, and so. The only thing left might be ideas or other highly abstract existents. Or even something that we can't conceive of in our present state." There is certainly no shortage of opinions on NDE/OBE. Even if we get past some claims that these phenomena are the result of misfirings of neurons or chemical changes in the brain, the world of science still can't definitively solve the spiritual aspects.

Another mystery I discuss in this book is that of those who claim to have psychic abilities and whether this is linked to the existence of the soul. Centuries ago, those who claimed to be able to tell the future, read the thoughts of others, or 'see' faraway locations were often said by others to be using magic or possessed by demons. Today, people still make these claims, such as mediums and remote viewers. Some see these phenomena as naturally legitimate, while others only see psi related activities through a religious lens and deny the possibility of people having these abilities without being possessed. I asked the doctor whether he thinks these phenomena could be real and should be tested scientifically. He reveals that "The Jewish medieval philosophers and commentators dealt with the occurrence of miraculous events as detailed in the Hebrew Bible. These include prediction, telepathy, and clairvoyance. There are instances of each scattered throughout the text. One of the ways in which they addressed this was by positing the existence of the Active Intellect. This is sometimes referred to as the lowest, or sublunar, sphere. This sphere regulates existence from the moon to the center of the earth. The highest sphere is closest to God, and lower spheres are contained within and influenced from above by the higher spheres. These intermediate spheres include those of the constellations, stars, and planets." The corresponding conceptual artwork and diagrams can actually be seen in various medieval pieces. Examples of this include Gossuin de Metz' "The Image of the World" (1245), Nicole Oresme's "Book of Heaven and Earth" (1377), and Domenico di Michelino's "The Comedy Illuminating Florence" (1456). It was believed that God, who had no need for physical form, could affect all physical and human movement throughout the spheres.

The Scientific Method

Strassman believes it could potentially be possible for someone to metaphysically establish a connection to the Active Intellect. He explains, "Since past, present, and future all exist within God's 'mind,' all knowledge of all possible outcomes also resides therein." A sensitive person who is able to reach a solid link to the Active Intellect can possibly get an inkling or revelation, which leads to the "possible outcome of future events, knowing what other people were thinking, or seeing things that the physical eyes were unable to". The above ideas describe the general thought process of medieval Jewish philosophers, who saw this as a way to explain miraculous occurrences. They often pushed aside explanations that had to do with magic or demons and claimed that those who used these reasons were unstable. The doctor posits that "This may have had as much to do with their interest in steering people toward a more rational approach to the Hebrew Bible and away from any pagan influence in one's interpretation of the text." It was not that these philosophers did not believe that magic and demons didn't exist, but that they wanted the faithful to focus on their relationship with God and their good standing with him. It was about adhering to God's word and avoiding self-centeredness.

Moving forward to modern times, phenomena labeled as paranormal have, at times, been looked at by the scientific community. According to Strassman, "Ian Stevenson's lab at the University of Virginia in the 1960s took the lead for many years." The late psychiatrist helmed research into children's recollections of past lives. He also looked into altered states, NDEs and other psychic activities. Strassman continues, "Rupert Sheldrake has more recently been applying scientific methodologies to psi and other phenomena. The Bems have recently published data suggesting that people are able to accurately predict the future in a carefully controlled scientific study." Daryl Bem, a professor of psychology emeritus at Cornell University, released his study in 2011 in the *American Psychological Association's Journal of Personality and Social Psychology*. The reaction was mixed, with many supporting the results of the research, while others categorically dismissed the study's evidence of ESP.

Strassman, who has many years of scientific research of his own under his belt, supports the study of seemingly unexplainable phenomena. He says, "Any phenomena within the natural world are capable of being examined by the scientific method. However, mechanisms do not necessarily translate into origins. That is, the proximal workings of the process under examination do not address how that process began. For example, one may understand how an arrow in the chest might cause bleeding, tissue damage, and death, but says nothing about who shot the arrow and why. The initiating process might be proximity to the Active Intellect or it might be of a more sinister demonic nature." Strassman concludes that, while observations can be made and data collected during studies of supposed paranormal activities, the question of *how* psi phenomena occur is still mysterious.

There are always medical cases in which physicians are doing their best to save a patient, and in the end there is some unexplained intervention. In Fall 2014, in Florida, a woman named Ruby was pregnant and undergoing a C-section at Boca Raton Regional Hospital. The baby was delivered, but unfortunately there was a complication with Ruby. She went unconscious and was unresponsive; during this time she had no pulse for 45 minutes! The staff attending her worked to bring her back for three hours. The doctor thought that she was not going to make it. He had to let her family know that while getting a healthy baby, they might lose Ruby. Out of

The Scientific Method

nowhere, there was an indication of a revived heartbeat on the monitor. She had come back to life! Later on, when talking with reporters, she said she had a near-death experience. She saw a spirit that she recalls being her deceased father. Ruby also said there was a light in the background and other beings present. Similar to other NDEs, she inferred from a "force" that it was not her time to go, and so she was sent back. The presiding physician, Dr. Chadi Loutfi, MD, told an ABC affiliate that this event was exceptional. He revealed, "The whole family and a big majority of the medical team believe there was at least some kind of divine intervention" ("Woman"). One doesn't always hear a doctor use the word "divine" in the medical field, but in the Hippocratic Oath it does mention that doctors should be willing to admit when they can't medically explain something. Of course, Ruby is just happy to be alive.

When doing research into the views of the scientific and medical community on whether there is existence after death, it is hard not to notice the growing number of doctors who relate stories from patients who clinically died for a short period of time and say they traveled to the other side. One of those present-day medical professionals is Dr. Jeffrey Long, who is a radiation oncologist and is the author of the book *Evidence of the Afterlife*. In 2010, he was interviewed by *Time* about his views of near death experiences based on his interactions with patients. In his view, there are so many theories about what NDEs are, from skeptics who include other doctors, because the supposed explanations don't really make sense. If there was one theory that made perfect sense then it could be the de-facto answer. He believes that what religious teachings have relayed to people over the years is being essentially proven by the experiences people have, and that it helps to bring the religious and scientific worlds closer on the subject of the afterlife. The interviewer asked Dr. Long about what makes his research so personal to him. He explained that he deals with sick patients with cancer, and he admits that not all of them can be saved. The important thing though is that because of his belief in an afterlife, he has more courage now to help his patients deal with a disease that threatens their earthly lives (Fitzpatrick). In fact, when it comes to experiences of people who die on the operating table and come back, there is a yearly meeting of medical and scientific minds to analyze the data. In 2006 the first International Medical Conference on Near-Death Experience took place in France. There was a group statement made that said there were chemical reactions in the brain during NDEs, but that there must be more to the story (Williams).

The greatest scientific reasoning in confirming the survival of our spirit is a well-known law of thermodynamics. The law was coined by Albert Einstein, saying "energy cannot be created or destroyed, it can only be changed from one form to another." This essentially means that one's spirit must go somewhere when their body dies. For those that already believe in the afterlife, this law translates into at least a couple of theories. Either the individual's soul has their intellect and memories intact, or as some believe, a person's energy simply folds into that of a universal one. In either scenario, an individual's intelligence ends up being part of the larger picture. Scientists will tell you that energy is all around us, all of the time. There are some forms of energy such as radio waves or infrared light that we can't see with the naked eye, but we know they exist.

Denial

For many scientists, academics, and medical experts, their skepticism or denial of the soul lies in their understanding of the human brain. In 2012, the short film *Neuroscience and the*

The Scientific Method

Soul was released by "The Research Group in Mind, Science and Culture"; this was an investigative project through the Liberal Arts & Sciences Department at Columbia College Chicago. The documentary starts off by pointing out that changes in philosophy occurred from the Egyptians, to the ancient Pre-Socratics of Greece, then the Pythagoreans, and on to Plato and his student Aristotle. Research team member Stephen T. Asma explains that the Pythagoreans thought that what others called the soul was really the workings of the physical brain. Yet, Plato was sure that when one died, a person could indeed survive without the body. He also saw the soul as being immortal and that we could carry our knowledge with us. However, his own student, Aristotle, disagreed with him. He said there were three types of soul: the nutritive, sensitive, and intellectual. He said that people are unique in having the latter. Unlike Plato, he thought that once we died, that was the end.

In continuing the discussion, team researcher Tom Greif says that early Greek and Roman philosophy had a great impact later on with Christian theologians. He points out that there was a mix of both Plato's and Aristotle's ideas in laying out the concept of the human soul. Greif explains that through doctrine composed by those such as St. Thomas Aquinas, people had an understanding that an immortal afterlife in connection with God was something that mattered greatly. He suggests that it makes sense that missionary work by the Christian Jesuits was taken seriously, because they were literally trying to save other people's souls. He goes on to say that hundreds of centuries later, when Charles Darwin introduced his Theory of Evolution, it would infer that all the previous ideas of the existence of the soul may be wrong.

Fellow researcher Rami Gabriel says that modern evolutionary theory and neuroscience have moved humanity forward in considering whether the soul exists. He explains that in analyzing how the brain works, scientists have proven that ideas about non-material capacities of a supposed soul do not exist. Gabriel says that the major parts of the human brain provide all the workings of what philosophers of the past said were accomplished by a supernatural soul. According to him, it's just gray matter and the current that runs through it.

Previous commentator Stephen T. Asma exclaims that even though some have dismissed the concept of the soul, many others still insist on it being reality. He thinks that in consideration of modern neuroscience, people can hold on to an updated concept of the soul; one that does not pertain to a mystical explanation. He says experiences in life that deeply affect people, such as moving music or love, are legitimate ways of expressing the "soulful" qualities of life.

Ultimately, the team agrees that the historical concept of the human soul is incorrect. Asma says that although we are in the modern age of science, "That doesn't mean, however, that we're left with nihilism; you know, the idea that nothing is meaningful" (Asma). He thinks that our core values as people give us meaning to life; to him, this is especially important in terms of our local area and our families. Greif expands this notion and explains that, considering our globally connected world, people should also be thinking of the needs of others. He says that it doesn't matter what country someone lives in, we all have common needs and values. The *meaning* that Asma mentions can take form in empathy for others both locally and planet-wide. In a final word, Gabriel also points out that we all share a common bond through art. He explains that people share an emotional connection to artwork, one that many would term as "spiritual". Gabriel says that while keeping in mind a brain-only approach, humanity can find deep meaning to life through art, but in a non-religious fashion.

The Scientific Method

There are numerous everyday occurrences that happen to people that may hint at the need for a 'spiritual intellect' that can reach beyond the physical body. Have you ever been by yourself–within your visual and audible range–and felt like there was someone near you and then someone showed up? This happens to a lot of people, but it's not clear how this feeling comes about. It could technically be possible that when indoors one is feeling slight vibrations through the floor. However, how strong those vibrations would have to be, or whether that indicates a human connection, is uncertain.

For over a century people have benefited from the use of telephones. It is common for people to say that they were thinking about a personal friend or family member, when soon after the phone rings and it is that person. Skeptics say that it is just a coincidence. If a person is close to hundreds of people who call them often, then it could be less of a happenstance. However, if one is used to only receiving five calls per week because they have few friends, it is more likely to just be a chance happening. Although this type of scenario seems anecdotal, there are also people who swear that they just *knew* that a certain person was calling.

As the years go by there are always new discoveries, or sometimes additions to older ones in the field of science. Recently there were some headlines in the news about scientific experiments in what is called quantum entanglement. The concept, which primarily came about via Einstein, basically is about photons or similar objects affecting other ones while they are completely separated. For instance, if two photons are used in an experiment that are originally together and then split apart, you could make one spin and the other one that is a mile away will also spin. Years ago, Einstein called this "spooky action at a distance." In many experiments used to illustrate entanglement, scientists use a laser beam that is then split into two separate beams, and there are usually light filters involved as well. There are indicators used to tell what is going on with pairs of photons, like speed or angles. You can tell what state the other particle is in from its "twin" or vice versa. There are now some scientists who are trying to figure out how entanglement can be integrated into what is called quantum computing. The concept is that in the future at some point this new technology will be used in place of what computers have now, so that the speed at which processes move is much faster. In commenting on an experiment by physicists at the University of Vienna, writer Jesse Emspak at *Live Science* online explains, "Though this transfer of information between the particles is instantaneous, entanglement can't be used for faster-than-light communication because it is impossible to set the quantum state beforehand, as you would in a message" (Emspak). Even still, if physicists could figure out a solid way to utilize manipulation of particles into quantum entanglement, it would certainly make the idea of computing as it is today obsolete. As far as sending data or instructions, we would never need anything faster than the speed of light anyways! In an article on *Scientific American* online, the author George Musser talks about an experiment he was a part of with others to show in a video what entanglement is all about. He mentions, "photons are acting in unison even though no known force or influence links them. And they do so despite being separated by the width of a hand, which, for an infrared photon, might as well be a million miles" (Musser).

So what does this have to do with the afterlife? Well as it turns out, it may be quite interconnected. Michael Shermer mentions in an article he wrote for *Skeptic.com*, that author Deepak Chopra supports something called quantum consciousness in his book *Life After Death: The Burden of Proof*. This is a theory that some other scientists and writers are

The Scientific Method

talking about as well. Shermer says, "Chopra takes this to mean that the universe is one giant quantum field in which everything (and everyone) is interconnected and can influence one another directly and instantly" (Chopra & Shermer).

There have been more general ideas like this for many years, but the theories lately have been getting more specific in terms of being linked with scientific properties. The basic idea behind this which is similar to quantum entanglement is that although it may seem like every physical object is separate from one another, they are really not. A more recent hypothesis, considering these quantum theories, is that every object leaves an identical copy of itself in the so called "giant quantum field." When somebody sees a ghost in a multi-story home and it is walking down a flight of stairs, is it really walking? Since the ghost lacks physicality, then perhaps it is stepping on the energy structure that the stairs have on the other side. Of course this is just a theory.

During an investigation by well-known American paranormal investigator John Zaffis, a client had Zaffis' team come to her property because her barn was haunted. The aim of the team was finding any objects which might have some connection to the haunting, which means that something would have happened in the past dealing directly with a certain physical object that was still around. In investigations of hauntings, there can sometimes be a piece of property left by a previous owner in a home, or it could be something buried in the dirt on the property for example. In this client's case, it turned out to be an old sharp tool that had been left in a toolbox in the barn from a previous owner. The way the team figured this out was that while combing the barn with a thermal imaging camera, the object, quite surprisingly, was glowing hot on the thermal readout, while all the other tools were cool like they would normally be. While considering the quantum theory mentioned, each tool should have a particle energy copy of itself in the astral dimension. Normally if nothing unusual, violent, or emotional happened in connection with an item, it would not glow hot on a normal thermal readout. The assumption by the team was that something had happened where the item was used in the past in some negative way; this is why it stood out and broke the normal laws of thermodynamics. Needless to say, more research needs to be done in the theory of quantum consciousness, as well as with quantum entanglement.

Speaking of quantum theory, the practice of remote viewing has been going on officially for over forty years. For those who are unfamiliar with the topic, remote viewing is when a person with psychic or extra-sensory-perception (ESP) abilities is able to see an assigned target in their mind from some distance away. Non-psychics have also been involved in this. Usually the viewer sees a series of images that, put together, forms an overall observation of a target; this is of an object, person, or geographical area that the viewer has not been told anything about. This person is given two sets of four digit numbers, which are picked after another person decides what the target will be. The remote viewer writes down the numbers, and tries to visualize what and where the target is, writes down key descriptions on a pre-formatted paper, as well as drawing what he or she sees. Many sessions are aimed at viewing something current, but it can also be in the past or even future. If it is in the past, it is called postcognition. When the target is in the future, it is called precognition.

The majority of people would probably find it surprising that the biggest supporter over the years of remote viewing, has been the U.S. government. In fact, according to Daz Smith, one of the most well-known remote viewers from the U.K., remote viewing was "developed for and utilized by The Department Of Defense for intelligence collection

The Scientific Method

purposes with the famed 'Star Gate' project, it has a long history (30+ years) as an intelligence gathering tool. Remote viewing started its long life and funding in 1972 and continued being funded for intel and research until 1995 when the secret projects were made public disclosure by the C.I.A and 'officially' closed" (Smith). Some of the top remote viewers who were contracted by the Department of Defense say that the program is still running, while other key players claim it is finished. Critics of the program claim that no real results came of it. One of the many people towing this line is famed scientist Michio Kaku. Apparently, if science can't prove remote viewing, then he doesn't believe it. The government originally started the program mainly to spy on Russia, their cold war foe, after discovering that the U.S.S.R. had their own remote viewing program. However, seeing things at a distance through the mind has had other uses as well; over the years it has been used to locate missing people, help solve crimes and mysteries, predict future terrorist attacks, describe planetary bodies prior to space satellite missions, locating medical problem areas for certain people, and much more.

Where this ties in to the concept of a soul within individuals is the distinct possibility that a soul is required for remote viewing. Looking at the practice of seeing from afar, in a purely scientific sense, one might question whether the brain alone could achieve this. After-all, the brain is just a big gray muscle in a skull. Of course a human mind is conscious, and people can do many great things with brain power. This book was typed on an advanced computer that can connect to wireless Internet; these things were thought up and created by smart individuals. If a team manager inside the C.I.A. could ask a remote viewer to tell him what is located at a certain set of coordinates, and it turns out to be a nuclear missile silo in Russia, what is enabling the person to see half-way around the world? The short answer is that everything is connected, and that the viewer's soul, interacting with space time, allows them to "visit" a remote target. They can glimpse appearances, and sometimes even sounds or smells. There have even been accounts from remote viewers who worked in the various government/military programs, saying they were spotted by someone in a past time, or in real-time by a counter-agent working in a foreign country. This means that their personal image was seen during a remote viewing session. This lends itself strongly to the probability of the requirement of the soul.

10

Time Flies
When You're Dead

"Time brings all things to pass."

- AESCHYLUS

WHEN YOU really think about what holds the seams of our day-to-day lives together, it must be one of the few constants of life. It is the glue that binds the days together, and its name is time. It lets us schedule when to eat dinner, or when to tune into a favorite TV show, or set an alarm clock. But what if time as we know it ceased to exist? People would be totally lost, because without the concept of a limited lifetime with only so many hours between sleep cycles, they could just sleep as much as they wanted to. Our sense of time as humans is formed in part based on our location in the solar system. The closer a planet is to the sun, the shorter it is for it to make a one year rotation. For instance, if we lived on the planet Mercury, it would only take 88 days to orbit the sun, which is only around 3 months. (Hitt) So in Earth years if you lived to be 88, on Mercury you would be 352! Of course it would be the same amount of actual time relatively speaking. But what about after those 88 years when your body grows tired and you move on to the hereafter?

There are numerous clues available to lead us in the right direction; clues that point to the idea that, in the great beyond, linear time does not exist. If we look at the environment in which we live, and attach Einstein's Special Theory of Relativity, we then understand that time is relative depending on the observer. Your view of the passing of time is affected by the speed at which you are moving. If you are standing on your front lawn, and throw a football to your friend that is fifty feet away, you will both observe the football moving at a judge-able rate. However, if another person drives by your front yard going forty miles-per-hour, the speed, to them, will appear a bit different. At the most extreme end of speed, scientists believe that nothing can move faster than the speed of light. We judge this speed by recording how long it takes light to reach the Earth from the Sun, which is around 186,000 miles per second. Now that's what I call fast!

In 1971, one of the greatest science experiments ever was undertaken by scientists J.C. Hafele and Richard E. Keating. They figured that based on Einstein's theory, if you were to travel in a jet-plane around the world that there would have to be some discrepancy in time between those in the air and those that were relatively stationary on the ground. "During October 1971, four cesium beam atomic clocks were flown on regularly scheduled commercial jet flights around the world twice, once eastward and once westward, to test Einstein's theory of relativity with macroscopic clocks. From the actual flight paths of each trip, the

Time Flies When You're Dead

theory predicts that the flying clocks, compared with reference clocks at the U.S. Naval Observatory, should have lost 40 ± 23 nanoseconds during the eastward trip, and should have gained 275 ± 21 nanoseconds during the westward trip" (Hafele & Keating). Their assumption was of course correct, as we have known for many years now. Later on in 1996, on the 25th anniversary of the Hafele/Keating flights, the experiment was recreated. A modern atomic clock was used which was more precise than the ones available in the 1970's. This time a roundtrip flight was undertaken between London and Washington D.C. The result, measured against atomic clocks on the ground, was a gain of 39 nanoseconds ("Einstein").

As humans, our view of linear time is fairly standard. The major difference between people on our planet is the time zones, because one half of the planet is always dark. When looking at the results of the tests of atomic clocks on jet flights, we notice that even though there is an irregularity of linear time, it is only miniscule. Consider that on a larger scale, the astronauts inside the International Space Station are orbiting around the planet at almost 18,000 mph. So if you are looking at a stay of many months, you are still only looking at a difference of milliseconds. But if you take into consideration that in the afterlife, its inhabitants are apparently made of energy, this starts to explain why time in the other dimensions would be non-linear. One of the first stages of NDEs is sometimes travel through a tunnel made of light and/or energy at great speed. Some people who report their experience say they sense that they go through the tunnel at the speed of light. Now the only sense people really have normally about how fast light can be, is when they flip a light-switch on or off. On a side-note, many people who report having an NDE say they were told by spirits or angels that in Heaven, time does not exist at all. This would seem to make sense because there wouldn't appear to be any reason to have time there. However, in the middle dimension, there definitely appears to be non-linear time, based on evidence collected in many ghost investigations. In fact, evidence includes voices being recorded mentioning historical events or years, investigators seeing ghosts dressed in old clothing such as the Victorian style, as well the living hearing old music being played. Clearly, ghosts are usually able to have two-way communication with the living, but one wonders whether they know all about events in time related to a certain location. Another part of this question is concerning whether the ghosts think we are in their time period, or if they can actually experience events past our own time into the far future.

One mind-bending feature of paranormal investigations is when the crew asks spirits to make a light turn on for energy meters or to speak into a recorder. The reality is, if you spoke to a ghost when it was living, let's say the person was from the mid 19th century, it would have no idea what those electronic devices were. The question becomes, do ghosts realize now what all the equipment is? If they do, then you begin to come to a realization that by crossing over and being folded into time itself, they may have received extended knowledge up to this point. This can begin to make sense when you encounter this concept in many NDEs, where people say that after traveling through the tunnel of light, they seem to gain all the knowledge they were missing in life. They say that life's great questions are answered and the big picture of a universal truth is suddenly known.

This coincides with non-linear time theory, and lends a hand in understanding future prophecies that come true. Our own view of time is part of the framework of space and time. How do we know this? If you look at the previously mentioned phenomenon of EVP recordings as well as spirit box communication, the responding answers are given to us in our time. That is to mean if a paranormal researcher is using a real-time spirit box device which pulls the voices out of the radio waves moving through the air, answers to questions correlate to our own time. However, we also know that the 'dimension' from which the voices are coming from is not exactly what we understand as our 'living' reality. According to some paranormal researchers, there are some ghosts that are in some kind of loop. For centuries, people have seen apparitions which appear every year but are always doing the same thing, like they walk from one room in a building looking in a certain direction, and then walk into another room and vanish. So every year or whatever time frame it is, the ghost just does the same thing over and over again. Looking at the theories in place today, there are two explanations for this. The first is that the apparition is an actual soul that is reliving its life to sort out deep problems, as some in eastern religion believe. The second theory is that the actual soul of the apparition is somewhere else, and what a living person sees is just a leftover energy engrained into the fabric of the space time continuum.

One of the most fascinating subjects in literature and motion picture over the past century and a half is that of time travel. Nowadays it is considered a blend between science-fiction and fact. There are now a handful of scientists and physicists around the world who are working on building real time machines. Some scientists think that it is in fact possible to time travel, but only to move forward and not backwards. When considering this topic, the majority of people probably don't think about its probable connection to the soul. This is an aspect of the theories that is not fully being explored at the moment. If you were able to travel back and not encounter anyone who was still alive from your time frame, it would have to be around 125 years to be safe. Now this would not mean that all questions are now answered. Things are still confusing. Where exactly is the essence of a person in your time frame who is gone, and are they still there when you see them when you go back in time? If you are walking down the street in London 150 years ago and you run into someone on the street, and have a conversation, is this person's soul current to their time frame? Of course, we as humans see time in a particular way, but if time is non-linear in other dimensions, could a soul be in different stages in various moments? It appears we will just have to wait and see until someone creates a real working time machine.

Rebirth

In Asia, one of the defining characteristics of religion has always been the belief in transmigration, the reincarnation of the soul. In Hinduism, Sikhism, and some other religions, it is said that soul lives many lives, while only stopping in the afterlife for a time in-between. Many Buddhists describe the concept as 'rebirth' without someone's consciousness being 'fixed'. Perhaps the best analogy of this would be that of using a flame to light another one, as the first one goes out. A being could be a prince, then a male soldier, then a female painter, and move on to become a biochemist. It is said that the being's next embodiment is chosen by itself and a higher power in the afterlife, and that the previous lifetime affects the choice. Some people who remember a past life believe a birthmark is sometimes a direct link to the previous body; it is perhaps a reflection of something that occurred to that section of the previous body. With Eastern religions, there is one spirit spanning time in different incarnations. Whereas, with Western religion, there is one eternal soul and a family bloodline going back in time.

In 204 AD, a boy was born in Egypt's Nile Delta region, which by that time was a province of the Roman Empire. He would become an influential philosopher named

Time Flies When You're Dead

Plotinus. Information about his life and teachings was recorded by his faithful student Porphyry. Plotinus was a fan of renowned thinker Plato, as were many others, basing his ideas on 'Platonism'. Today, Plotinus is credited with starting 'Neo-Platonism'. When he was nearing the age of 40, he had the opportunity travel with a Roman military expedition that would move east towards India. He wanted to find out how the great philosophers thought in that region of the world. Unfortunately things went south—figuratively speaking—and he had to flee west. He went to Rome and decided to stay there, where he taught his style of philosophy.

Before his ill-fated trip, Plotinus was studying texts in Alexandria, Egypt, home to the great Library at Alexandria. The famous library was damaged numerous times over the centuries until being destroyed in the 7th century. The philosopher believed in the soul and that it was the reason for desire. He also believed the soul was not temporary. In fact, he concluded, as did the Indian philosophers, that souls are reincarnated. His view of this process would parallel that of many modern Asian religions (Law).

Recollections and conceptions of previous lives are not limited to Asia or Africa; they also occur in Western countries as well. One of the most famous American military leaders, General George S. Patton, was a believer in past lives. He felt that his destiny had always been to lead soldiers on the battlefield. In fact, he believed he was a reincarnation of the second century Carthaginian general Hannibal, who fought the Roman Empire. Patton loved to write poetry, which may be surprising to some, considering his tough-guy image. He not only served in WWII, but also in WWI. In 1922 he wrote a poem entitled "Through a Glass Darkly", in which he expresses his beliefs. Here are just two of the poem's stanzas: *"So as through a glass and darkly / The age long strife I see / Where I fought in many guises, / Many names – but always me." "So forever in the future / Shall I battle as of yore, / Dying to be born a fighter / But to die again once more"* ("Through"). Patton's memory of fighting in the past was alluded to in the biographical war film *Patton* from 1970.

In the episode "Previous Lives" of the BBC Learning documentary series *Supernatural Science*, the stories of individuals around the world who recalled past lives were presented. As is revealed in the documentary, oftentimes it is a young child who has recollections, while sometimes it begins as an adult. The show started off visiting American Patricia Austrian, and her family in Connecticut. She related the memories that her son, a teenager at filming, had when he was a small child. She said starting at one year old, he feared dark rainy days, and that they made him apprehensive. Her son Edward was often sick, and developed a cyst in his throat by age four. When talking with his parents about it, he referred to the spot on his throat as his 'shot'. Doctors planned a surgery, but decided to remove his tonsils beforehand. After this initial operation, Edward related a story of his past life to his mother, while in the hospital. Patricia was shocked to hear a gripping ordeal of him being a WWI soldier in France; paraphrasing, she said, "We were walking along through the mud. It was damp, it was raining, it was cold, my rifle is heavy. I remember looking out and seeing fields of trees, and then there was desolation. I heard a shot come from behind, and it went through someone else, hit me square in the back of the neck, and I felt my throat fill with blood" (netholer). These were the type of details of war that a four year old should not be aware of. Edward's father, a doctor, was not sure what to think of the story. He, the family, and their son's hospital doctor, were amazed when the cyst simply vanished! At that point, his parents became convinced there was a connection, and believed him.

Another individual featured in the documentary was Bruce Whittier, a man from Nova Scotia, Canada. As an adult, out of the blue, he started having a series of dreams every night, which seemed to be memories from another lifetime. He remembered seeing a man he didn't know, hiding inside a building. Then he realized he was also hiding, that he had a family, and they were fearful. He started writing down what happened in his dreams into a journal. He points out a drawing he made of pendulum clock, and says it was on a table in the room he was hiding in. At first he didn't understand what was going on, but started to realize that he and everyone else were Jews, hiding from the Nazis in WWII. In the vivid dream recollections, they were eventually found by Nazi officers, were put on a train, and sent to the Auschwitz concentration camp. Whittier, as his current self, is not Jewish. In a strange twist, he saw in one of his dreams where he could locate the clock he saw; it apparently was still around. He struggled over whether to go to the location, for weeks. Finally he decided to go to the shop he saw in his dream, which turned out to be an antiques store in Nova Scotia. He walked into the shop, and there was the clock. The store owner said he had acquired it on a trip to Europe, while in Holland. He said clock had been owned by a German military officer.

The producers of "Previous Lives" also filmed some subjects in the country of Sri Lanka, the island nation underneath India. They first met with a couple who have a daughter, Chathurika, who appears to be around eight years old. The girl started to have memories of what she said was a past life when she was three years old. She claimed to recognize the members of a nearby family from her previous life. Chathurika believed that in her last incarnation, she was Siriyawathi. The girl had never had the chance to meet her because the woman died at the age of thirty-five. The girl told the family the details of their mother's death; that she was struck and killed by a van. Her recollection was correct, even though no one had told her of this. Siriyawathi's children are now adults, at least in their twenties. The girl took a ride with the family members down a road, and when they got to a certain point, she made the connection. She recognized it as the spot of the accident, where Siriyawathi died, and she wept.

Another child in Sri Lanka was also featured in the documentary. A boy named Chatura Karunaratne had told his parents, at three years old, that their house was not his real home. He told them of his parents before that time, and that he was from Narammala, a town nearby. He recalled being a soldier who was with others traveling in a truck, and that they ran over a land-mine. He recalled getting thrown out of the vehicle and into the ditch along the road, and then being shot. Chatura also remembered his right arm being broken, and that he was shot under his left ear in the town of Trincomalee. It is relevant to mention that there was a civil war in the country between 1983 and 2009. His parents had a local journalist stop by their home to write an article for the paper, because they wanted to locate the family from that town who had lost a son in that particular manner. Posting articles of past life remembrances is a common practice in Sri Lanka. A married couple from Narammala, perhaps in their sixties, read the article in the newspaper. They were surprised the story matched that of their son, Dayananda, who died at nineteen in the civil war. The father said that his son was the only one to die from his area in that attack. The details that the boy had recalled were a match for the dead soldier. Chatura had also said that his father in his previous life was a bricklayer, and that he (Dayananda), had run some kind of shop. These additional recollections turned out to also be true. The older couple made contact, and Chatura and his parents went to visit them. Upon recognizing them, with teary eyes, he called them mother and father.

11

Ghost in the Machine

> "Thou shalt not make a machine to counterfeit a human mind."[19]
>
> - FRANK HERBERT, *Dune*

FOR MANY YEARS, scientists and inventors have considered the possibilities of creating artificial people. In general, most of the mechanical human-like robots have been fairly rudimentary. However, during the last decade, the technology and materials available have progressed quite a bit. There are a handful of current androids that look human, and even have full size bodies. Some people have concerns over the purposeful humanization of what are essentially robots. According to a concept known as "uncanny valley", people are sometimes uncomfortable at the sight of a near perfect moving simulation of a

---

[19] "Artificial" (See Bibliography)

human face. According to a detailed article on this subject by the BBC, almost 45 years ago Japanese roboticist Masahiro Mori published a paper in the academic journal *Energy*, introducing the idea. He called it "Bukimi No Tani", which "only roughly translates into the phrase it has made famous. A more accurate translation is 'valley of eeriness'" (Eveleth). The BBC piece mentions the CGI movie *Final Fantasy: The Spirits Within* as an example of the phenomenon, pointing out that the film tanked at the box-office. I personally went to see the movie at the theater, and recall being impressed by the amazing graphics, which fourteen years ago were groundbreaking. Just as others did, I noticed the soulless look in the character's gazes.

In 2005 one of the world's preeminent roboticists, Professor Hiroshi Ishiguro, created the geminoid HI-1. The initials represent the creator's name, and the geminoids are a series of telepresence robots which are modeled after specific people. Ishiguro works in the Department of Systems Innovations within the Graduate School of Engineering Science, inside Osaka University in Japan. The robots were created so that a person could, in a way, be present in more than one location at a time. The geminoids cannot walk, so they are always seated. If a person worked for a multinational corporation that held meetings between countries, they could have their own geminoid in another nation, and would remotely control the head and facial movements, as well as speaking through it. It can also be used for individuals who are involved in annual conventions; if they cannot be there in person, they could speak through their humanoid robot to the audience. The geminoids look very realistic, and have skin made from silicone; however, people can tell that they are not real. There are now four versions of the professor's replicant robot, and two other geminoids as well; one is of a real Japanese woman, and the other is molded after an actual man in Denmark.

Ghost in the Machine

In explaining the goals of the geminoids project, Ishiguro has talked about the Japanese term "Sonzai-Kan". This is the concept of the android containing the "presence", or as the professor also words it, the "authority" of the individual it represents (Ishiguro). Areas of focus for the professor and his team have been the geminoid's speech sound, moving lips, emotional expressions, and moving eyes that track human faces. This cannot be considered the equal of a soul, but more like an interactive shell of a real person. The real question at hand is whether people can feel almost the same way they do talking with the actual individual. Obviously robots like the geminoids have a long way to go in terms of realism, but what if they become *too* advanced? As the ten year anniversary of the release of the first geminoid approaches, there are some who already feel the androids are just too creepy.

Another android that has captured attention in recent years is the HRP-4C "Miim". It was created in Japan by the AIST corporation, introduced in 2009, and is modeled on the average figure of young Japanese women. Unlike the geminoid robots, this design can actually walk around, mimic general human movement, and even dance! It can also talk and sing. The walking has been improved over the years, and is now appears fairly realistic. Its head looks human, but not the rest of the body. It is the only humanoid robot this advanced, in terms of mobility, in the entire world. This is not a purely telepresence robot, it uses speech recognition software and vocal processing to talk.

In taking a final look at androids of today, there is a model made by Hanson Robotics in America, which is different from the other two already mentioned. It is a replica of the late author Philip K. Dick, who wrote *Do Androids Dream of Electric Sheep*, which was the basis for the 1982 sci-fi movie *Blade Runner*. Dick passed away that same year. The main focus for this project has been on the conversation and software side. The company is attempting to form the beginnings of artificial intelligence with this android. As of now, it has a full body that is seated, just for appearance, and the head is the only active piece. There are many moving parts that give the robot facial expressions and the ability to move its mouth while talking. It can also turn its head and use facial recognition technology to look at people. The replica of the author utilizes a word and phrase database, information online, and 'learn' new things by talking to people. In a 2011 documentary by Nova on PBS, entitled *NOVA ScienceNOW: What's the Next Big Thing? - Social Robots*, commentator Chad Cohen sat down for a chat with the android. Cohen seemed surprised by how life-like the face was, and wanted to test the communication skills of the robotic duplicate. Cohen complimented "Philip" on his nice appearance. The humanoid robot responded by saying "Um… you're starting to over-inflate my ego, but don't let me stop you" ("NOVA"). With that, Cohen laughed out loud.

Reviewing all three humanoid robots, clearly they each have design focuses. The geminoid series is about communication between a human host, through an android head, with other people. The HRP-4C is the clear standout for testing androids that will, in the future, walk alongside humans in buildings and on the streets. Finally, Hanson Robotics' PKD robot is on the cutting edge of the push for artificial intelligence; this is probably the most important aspect of android development. Obviously in looking at the big picture, the idea is that in the future these three model types would be integrated into one amazing android. The next step would be what Google's Director of Engineering Ray Kurzweil talks a lot about: the "singularity". This refers to the point at which a computer, perhaps an android, becomes self-aware via real artificial intelligence. For people who are very weary of this occurring, they usually make references to the *Terminator* movies. In his recent book *Physics*

Ghost in the Machine

of the Impossible author and famed scientist Michio Kaku proclaims, "There is no universal consensus as to whether machines can be conscious" (121). Hypothetically, let's say that in twenty years full artificial intelligence goes live in an android. If an AI android starts making all of its own decisions, what if its creators disagree with it? Does the artificial being have any rights? Does this mean it has some kind of "electric spirit", or a digitally-based soul?

In the movie *A.I. Artificial Intelligence*, a 2001 release from director Steven Spielberg, androids and humans share the world. The artificial people are referred to as "mechas", and they did not have as many rights as humans. A couple, Monica and Henry Swinton, have a boy who has a terminal illness. The doctors don't have a way to save him at that moment, so the child is put in a cryogenic suspended animation. Henry works at a company that has developed cybernetic kids that can become a part of regular families. One day Henry surprises his wife by bringing home one of these child mechas. Her reaction was not entirely favorable, and her husband is not happy because he feels he is just doing the right thing. He convinces her to just give it a chance, so he stays, and he gets the name David. He sometimes seems normal, while conversely he has odd reactions or misunderstandings. Eventually Monica rejects him, after her real son was able to be treated, and has come home. One day Monica takes David for a drive, stops her car, and abandons him in the woods. The robot boy tried to please his "mother", but she could not make a place for him in her heart. He seemed to lack the essence of what it is to be human. David was designed for a purpose, and could learn about the world, while appearing to be a boy. At the end of the movie, David is found under the ocean in New York City, 2,000 years later during the next ice age, by advanced beings. They are the mecha of the future, and have outlasted humanity. If they were asked whether they had souls, it's anyone's guess as to what they would say.

Within the world of Japanese anime, the *Ghost in the Shell* TV series and movies are among the most well-known. The first movie debuted in 1996, and the multiple story-lines take place in the 2020s and 2030s. It is a dystopian world, where there are technologically-enhanced humans, and robots called "dolls" that contain the essence of individuals within them. If a robot doll becomes damaged, and is not useable any longer, the 'person' who inhabits it can be put into a new doll. The biggest types of crime in this future time are cyber-terrorism and data theft. In a reference to the film *Ghost in the Shell 2: Innocence*, the director Mamoru Oshii stated in an interview at DreamWorks studio that the movie "concludes that all forms of life—humans, animals, and robots—are equal" (Hart). He went on to talk about the need for people of today to change their ways, because things are going in a negative direction. It seems that within the universe of *Ghost in the Shell*, the human soul is also valid inside an artificial body. What that means for humanity is something Oshii wants viewers to think about.

Now one of the top sci-fi cult classics, the film *Blade Runner* was released in 1982. It starred Harrison Ford, Rutger Hauer, Sean Young, and Edward James Olmos, among many others. The movie took place in 2019, which is only four years from the time of this writing. It was set in a cyberpunk dystopian Los Angeles that was dark and polluted. There were clones of humans that were designed and grown by the Tyrell Corporation, which was helmed by a brilliant scientist of the same name. These androids with artificial intelligence were programmed with short lifespans of around four years, and were called "replicants". Their brains were infused with memories of real individuals, so that they would feel like they were human. They were simply made to do work at various jobs which are "off-world", which means on another planetary body. Dr. Tyrell had created various generations of replicants, and these were the sixth iteration. The replicants creator, Tyrell, said his companies' motto is "more human than human" ("Blade Runner"). If, as in the case of the storyline, replicants sneak back to Earth, then they are hunted down by "blade runners", which are a special police unit. The replicants look totally normal, and can blend right in with humans. The Tyrell Corporation realized that because these android models were so advanced, they had to institute the lifetime limits, because they might start producing their own emotions. The main character, Deckard, is a blade runner. He ends up falling in love with one of the female replicants he is told to 'kill'. By the end of the movie, Deckard, played by Harrison Ford, realizes that he may also be a replicant! This film blurred the lines between human and not-human. When a blade runner hunted down and eliminated a fugitive replicant, did the android go to some kind of afterlife? It would be difficult, after watching the movie, to say the replicants didn't have some kind of 'essence' within them.

One of the most recent films to deal with the issue of artificial intelligence, was 2014's *Transcendence*, starring Johnny Depp and Morgan Freeman. Depp plays Dr. Will Caster, who is considered the top expert in the world on artificial intelligence. The scientist is trying to finish a program that will be self-aware, understand human emotion, and utilize the collective intelligence of the internet. There is an organized group of people who are opposed to his work, and fear it will lead to something harmful to the population. The group poisons the doctor with radiation, which ends up backfiring. While he is mortally injured, he, his wife, and a coworker, decide to upload his mind to the computer. Will Caster passes away, but the computer transfer is a success. He is now a fully digital consciousness, who has access to all available knowledge. The digital Caster now starts to work on solving problems of the world, and inventing new things. At first his wife is pleased that she can still communicate with him, but she starts to realize that his personality is starting to change, and so do others. Caster finds ways to heal the sick and broken, using nanotechnology. But he can also control their minds! Many people, including the government, realize he is altering human beings, and that things have progressed too far. The doctor's adversaries decide that he is too powerful and must be eliminated; Caster must die a second death.

One of the questions the film brings to mind is whether the scientist's soul was a part of the computer transfer, or if it is was simply an intelligence. One of the interesting twists of the story is at the end of the movie; Caster figures out how to use nanotechnology to recreate his body, and downloads himself into it. But is the spark of life inside this duplicated body? He comes off as unemotional and detached, and it is clear that something is missing. Perhaps only the memories and brainpower of the individual can really be digitally transferred.

The aforementioned Ray Kurzweil is, in some ways, like the fictional Dr. Caster. Both men are scientists who work to achieve artificial intelligence. An immense drive is a shared trait between them. Kurzweil believes, as did Caster, that he will actually live forever, one way or another. As was reported in an article about him and his job at Google in *The Guardian* newspaper, "he takes 150 pills a day" and has himself injected with various vitamins and supplements, among other things (Cadwalladr). He feels that this regiment he has put together will lengthen his lifespan, and that it can work for others in his generation as well. He sees medical technology and science changing all the time and thinks that monumental discoveries will occur over the coming decades which will help him and others attain long life. Even if he never makes it past 100, he has mentioned in his writing the concept of transferring a human mind and conscience into a digital format; he argues that this would be a way for someone to survive without the biological component. As one would expect, there are those who question Kurzweil's thinking, in terms of whether the 'spark' of life can actually be put into a computer. He is one of the leaders of the worldwide transhumanism movement, whose followers believe that humanity can move on from being biological entities and achieve immortality through cybernetics or virtual bodies. In 2013, Kurzweil spoke at the 2nd Global Future 2045 International Congress in NYC, whose mission is "to ensure the survival of civilization, build a bright future for all mankind, reach new goals and create new meanings and values for a humane, ethical, and high-tech future". He said that by 2045 the brain-computer interface will be figured out so that the vision he and others have will come true.

There are certainly numerous issues surrounding the digital mind transference theory, as well as vastly lengthened lifespans. Would most people even want to live past 100 years old? What about quality of life? Today, some people who make it into their 90s or more are doing relatively well. Yet, for others, they are wheelchair-bound or cannot get out of bed. Even if people started integrating cybernetics into their bodies, it is largely unknown how they would be viewed by the public at large. Today, one occasionally sees someone walking around with an advanced prosthetic that is wired to the brain. But there is some underlying need for it, as in war veterans or someone who was in a horrible car crash. These are not elderly people who live in nursing homes who decided to try and cheat death. As far as 'moving' one's mind (or 'self') into a computer or synthetic body, whether this could be achieved in the future is unknown. For atheists, the problem of the unseeable soul is not part of the equation, so it is just an issue of brainwaves and memory. For others, it seems almost impossible that 100% of the self could be transferred into something that is not biological. Even if this were possible, could one's 'data' be hacked? Could someone maliciously delete or edit part of your 'file'? At this point, it's all up in the air.

Epilogue:
The Path Ahead

"The future starts today, not tomorrow."

- POPE JOHN PAUL II

TODAY, even with all the data and knowledge that is one keystroke away, it is difficult to wade through all of it to come to an agreement on what the spirit, soul, or afterlife is. In light of how we as humans decipher facts and opinions about the unknown, the information becomes relative to different degrees. For instance, a minority of scientists agree that people have a soul made of energy and that it goes into some kind of conscious afterlife. Other scientists think that whatever energy is part of a person will become part of the environment in some way to be recycled, but that the person's knowledge and identity will be lost. You can have both groups, with similar degrees in science, come to different conclusions using the same information. Let's look at a fictional example: three students at a New York City university. They are all English majors, but one is Buddhist, one Protestant, and the other Atheist. They all have a similar life at school and are the same age, but because of their beliefs they will disagree on the issues of the spiritual and the afterlife.

Speaking of not seeing eye to eye, as I got ready to send this book to the Editor, I happened to come across an interesting find. I was casually perusing the new books section in my local bookstore when one title caught my eye; it had the word 'soul' in it. Well perhaps it was not *that* soul, maybe it was soul food or soul music. Nope. Alas, it was the same soul that my own book refers to. In fact, it was *The Soul Fallacy: What Science Shows We Gain From Letting Go of Our Soul Beliefs*. The book, authored by Julien Musolino, was put out only months before my own book was to be finished. Admittedly, my first thought was, "He beat me to it!" Considering that his book is, in some ways, the opposite of mine, my second thought was, "Great, now I can better understand the contrary viewpoint!" I definitely explored many fascinating books while doing research for my own, but this one was particularly unique.

Musolino, according to his author bio, is a "cognitive scientist and an associate professor at Rutgers University, where he directs the Psycholinguistics Laboratory and holds a dual appointment in the Department of Psychology and the internationally renowned Center for Cognitive Science". Due to the type of work the professor is involved with, he has come to an apparently inevitable conclusion; the longstanding belief, held by most people, that the soul is a part of us, is a big lie! Yes, a professor at a Northeast university has said that religion is wrong about something. Ok, so maybe this is not surprising. And before any web sleuths track down my resume, let me be the first to disclose that I went to a liberal arts college in Boston. In fact, I have no problem with

The Path Ahead

universities in this region, and I believe they are some of the best in the world. It should come as no surprise that the professor, who deals with the human mind, should think that our consciousness is simply our brain. In *The Soul Fallacy*, Musolino talks a lot about recent popular books which espouse a view opposite to his. He takes a particular handful of authors to task, especially Dinesh D'Souza and that author's book *Life After Death: The Evidence* (2009). That particular title comes from a Christian perspective, and covers NDEs, brain science, biology, physics, and philosophy.

From the start, the professor explains that he faces an uphill battle in his bid to convince people that the soul does not exist. In fact, during his research he found out that the majority of his own students at Rutgers disagree with him! This would seem somewhat awkward, but he soldiers on anyways. In his book, he labels his opponents, authors who are sure that science is compatible with the soul, as 'new dualists'. The latter part generally refers to those who agree that there is both a physical brain and a spiritual aspect. To be fair, Musolino says he hopes people from both sides of the argument will read his book, and that it is good to understand the viewpoints of both. I certainly agree.

Musolino posits that if what New Dualists believe is true, that there is a soul that can detach from the body, then there should be a provable avenue of communication with the 'dead'. This would be a testable event, one that would satisfy the scientific community. Even though he can't bring himself to admit it, Electronic Voice Phenomenon (EVP) meets this requirement. Voice recorders, which range from cheap to expensive, can be purchased by anyone. Scientists fully understand how these devices work. Any self-respecting paranormal investigation group, as I covered earlier in this book, will have at least one of these on hand. The recorder will either be new or be used with blank recording space on it. Some may question whether there is an issue with using a recorder which still has recordings on it. However, the device is always going to record a new file; it is not mixing a new event with an old, or at least not on top of it. It is actually easy to prove the existence of spirit voices using voice recorders. When a team brings one in, usually digital but sometimes tape, they already know how many people are there in a lockdown location. If there are five people, then obviously you would expect to hear no more than five distinct voice patterns on the recordings. If the team gets extra voices on a new recorder, which oftentimes happens, then the "proof is in the pudding". How could Musolino or anyone else deny this? Now sometimes, there are issues of voice spillage from nearby. There could be someone walking just outside the wall of the building. Sometimes investigation teams explore housing, so if people are in abutting home unit, this is something that needs to be taken into consideration. However, in the case of a building that is not near any others, there should not be an issue.

Another topic the professor touches on is *psi*. This has to do with psychic phenomena like precognition. He says there is simply nothing to it. Yet again, he is quick to ignore evidence which helps back up the existence of the spiritual. As mentioned in a previous chapter, the US government was involved in psychic warfare during the Cold War. In fact, it wasn't *our* idea at the start, it was the Soviets. The KGB, Russia's former intelligence agency (where current Russian President Vladimir Putin worked) knew of powerful psychics in their midst and employed them to spy on America from a distance. Their handlers had them remote-view places like missile silos, agency offices, and military outposts. The US government and military intelligence found this to be credible and copied the Russians. This went on for around three decades (secretly paid for by the taxpayers). Talk about a pile of evidence!

The Path Ahead

Finally, in *The Soul Fallacy* the author makes it a point to contrast the citizenry of the US with others, like many European countries. He reveals that according to major polling, Americans tend to hold strong religious beliefs. Compared to most other developed countries, he claims that this state of affairs is 'excessive'. The majority of Americans believe in God, the afterlife, souls, angels and demons. He essentially contends that the super-religious in the US are trying to kill Darwin in his grave. Yet, Musolino seems to want to avoid certain truths. The reality is that we are a melting pot and there are people here who hold all sorts of beliefs. This country is home to just about every religion on the planet. Of course, to an atheist, none of that matters. Also, this country was, in part, founded by those who sought religious freedom. Not only were they feeling oppressed, but the British refused to let them go for many decades. Of course, this doesn't prove whether the soul exists, but the history matters. It helps make America what it is today.

In this technological age we live in, people are starting to ask questions about the growing importance of the digital aspect to their lives. For instance, how will your profile on a social network be handled after you die? You may have joined a site ten years earlier, uploaded thousands of photos, and then got into a freak auto accident. To you, those photos, or at least the ones that aren't embarrassing, are important. They are the digital version of an old physical photo album that you would normally pass on to your family. Of course, there are other virtual belongings that might be important to you as well, such as home videos, self-produced music, or academic writings. There are now some businesses that handle this digital afterlife process for you and you just have to plan how it will be done before you pass away.

There are also some social media sites that are starting to think about how to integrate this after-death planning into their sites for their users, for instance companies like Google. According to a recent article from the *Washington Post*, Google has now included a tool in account settings called the Inactive Account Manager. This new tool is not exclusively there in case you pass away; it would be implemented if you were away for too long, like you got arrested and were sentenced to ten years in jail. If you did not have someone you knew to watch your account for you, it would eventually be deleted. It says in the news article that "those who use the Inactive Account Manager can choose to have their data deleted three, six, nine, or twelve months after it becomes inactive" (Tsukayama). If you wanted someone in your family to be given your account upon your passing, you can set that up. For a company like Google, this can include email, a blog, picture albums, notes, Youtube account, and even your online VOIP phone number with voicemails. Of course there are things to think about before an account(s) is considered for transfer, like emails or voicemails that you would not want a certain family member to know about. After considering the growing digital aspect of our lives, we basically end up in contemplation of the same kind of ideas our ancestors have had for centuries. What kind of person did people think I was? Did those who knew me view me as a nice or mean person? Who should I leave my home to? These are some of the basic questions that become relevant to us when it's all over.

Today, when thinking about the concept of life after death, the topic of ghosts is as important as ever. One thing people should take into account is if they have seen a ghost materialize, when they were just minding their own business, then they have caught a glimpse of the afterlife while they were still alive. Some people would argue that in a percentage of hauntings, what others might see are actually demons

The Path Ahead

disguised as humans or energy imprints from spirits. After all the evidence over the centuries, especially in the last few decades, it should be fair to say that if you were not expecting to see a ghost and did not ask a spirit to appear, then you saw a real ghost. In most cases this happens when someone is in their home, for instance watching television, and an apparition fades into view and then goes through a wall and dissipates. In applying such an experience to one's self, an individual should understand that an apparition is a symbol of only part of the afterlife world. There will always be more to the story that the human mind cannot fully grasp.

With talk of the world beyond, sometimes there is not enough focus on the here and now. In all major religious beliefs, you will find the concept of right and wrong, and of consequences for actions. The way down the right path, which continues past human existence, is and always will be taught in different ways. There are those figures in history who have led people and were, in return, admired by them, and who also left their thoughts for posterity. One leader, probably the most famous U.S. President, Abraham Lincoln, said in an 1862 message to Congress that "In times like the present, men should utter nothing for which they would not willingly be responsible through time and eternity" (Basler). Lincoln certainly had a lot on his shoulders and had to constantly make important decisions that would affect others during his term, and after he had died. Another U.S. President, Franklin D. Roosevelt, once said that "If you treat people right they will treat you right – ninety percent of the time" (Rosenberg). You can deal with people you meet in the way you know is right, even if you're sure that a small percent of those you encounter are wrong-headed.

Some people believe that your words and decisions will become engrained into an invisible cloud of infinite knowledge, which is updated instantaneously. There are various names for this including The Akashic Records, The Book of

Life, and the Hall of Records. It is said that once you say something, it is permanently in the record for eternity, and you cannot erase or change it. This ties into the idea of how you treat other beings throughout your life, also recognized as karma in the East. The statements, decisions, and actions are sewn together into the fabric of space and time. In particular, each person and object in our world is made of matter and energy, and is almost like a complex computer code. Sometimes various 'codes' affect other ones in positive or negative ways, but we as people don't always realize it. In some ways a city full of human interaction is akin to an ecosystem in a nature preserve. You may make a decision which has a link to morality that ends up affecting someone else you have not even met. Science tells us that "for every action there is an equal and opposite reaction." You might find out that your best friend is a drug dealer and they're selling to teenagers in your neighborhood. You make an anonymous call to the police and your friend is arrested and sentenced to fifteen years in prison. It seems you made the right decision. However, now his three kids are left with their mother, who is an alcoholic and can't keep down a job to pay for expenses. The kids end up bouncing from home to home, facing one hardship after another. Your decision to report your friend is now, perhaps, not so clear. On the other hand, it's possible that at least one of those kids will grow up to become a community leader and mentor to disadvantaged kids. How scenarios like this affect what occurs in the hereafter is not completely known.

Even looking at a normal everyday decision related to supply and demand we can see the basic principle. Let's say you go to the supermarket and see some organic papaya from Hawaii for sale, so you bag some. Let's back up nine months before you made the purchase. The farm owner hires an extra hand at the start of the season, and this person works on seeding and irrigation. Another worker goes out to the plants months later to pick the fruit. Once they are collected together, a third person packs them in small crates. A truck driver comes out to the farm and loads them up. The crates arrive at a national shipping company, and a loader puts them onto an airplane. The pilot lands in San Francisco, and another company worker brings them into the receiving facility. Someone from the airport checks to make sure the crates look ok and that they are what they are supposed to be. Then another truck driver loads them onto a semi bound for the supermarket. The papayas get there and someone working in the back puts them in the section of the back warehouse. A worker from the floor cleans them off and puts them out in the display in the vegetable and fruit section of the store. You walk by and pick them out. Wow! I'm sure I must be missing a couple people in there, but you get the point. You just helped eleven people to make a living and pay their bills! It was all affected by that one decision and those from others like you. When considering the afterlife, think of how you have treated others in this life, and the interpersonal decisions you have made over the years.

In seeking the truth of what lies beyond the barrier between our stage of life and the next, you have already completed the first step. You have chosen to expand your knowledge of the beliefs of others, through this overview of all the key components to the spirit, soul and afterlife. The next step is to look further into each piece of the puzzle: science, time & space theories, paranormal evidence, near death experiences, and religion. Once you are satisfied with your conclusions for each component, you will form your own complete idea of what is true. Along your travels, you may talk with others about the spiritual and tell them what you believe they can expect on the other side. Then, the only thing left to do is to convince them of why you are right and they are wrong. Or is it the other way around? Either way, remember that the quest for knowledge never ends.

Acknowledgments

The topics contained within these pages are both wide-ranging and multifaceted. Without the kind and gracious support from the following interviewees, I would never have been able to complete this book:

Harpreet Singh, Ph.D

Chaplain Swami Tyagananda

Marcel Poorthuis, Ph.D

Mohamed Ibrahim, Ph.D

Han Nee Lim, MA

Rick J. Strassman, M.D.

Grand Master Jong Soo Lee
with Master Linda Lee

Alongside the experts I had the pleasure of interviewing, I must also recognize the following people:

Editor Jeff O'Brien

Copy Editor Rachel C. Meehan

Carl, a former co-worker; one of my greatest boosters over my years of writing this book.

Note: The views and findings expressed in this book are those of the author, and do not necessarily reflect those of these individuals.

Bibliography

"2003,1022,0.11." *British Museum Asia Collection Database*. British Museum, 30 Aug. 2014. Web.

Alighieri, Dante. *Inferno*. Ch. 5. Trans. James Romanes Sibbald. Edinburgh: David Douglas (Edinburgh University Press), 1884. Kindle version. Public Domain. Dec 18, 2012. Web.

"al-Kindi." *Islamic Philosophy Online Project*. Islamic Philosophy Online, Inc., 19 Jan. 2008. Web.

"And Never the Twain Shall Tweet." *Questionable Quotes*. Snopes.com, 26 Sep. 2007. Web.

Anissimov, Michael. "What are Shadow People?" *wiseGeek*. Conjecture Corporation, 11 Jun. 2014. Web.

"Antoninus Pius." *Illustrated History of the Roman Empire*. Roman-Empire.net, n.d. Web.

"Archangel." 2013. *Wikipedia*. Wikimedia Foundation, 2013. Web.

"Artificial Intelligence Quotes." *Notable Quotes*. Notable-Quotes.com, 2014. Web.

Ash, Thomas. "The Case Against The Cosmological Argument." *Atheist Ground*. Big Issue Ground, 2001. Web.

Asma, Stephen. "Neuroscience and the Soul (The Research Group In Mind, Science and Culture --Columbia College Chicago, LAS)." Online video clip. *Vimeo*. 11 Oct. 2012. Web.

Atwater, P. M.H. "Ch. 11: Integration." *Near-Death Experiences, The Rest of the Story: What They Teach Us About Living, Dying, and Our True Purpose*. New York: MJF, 2011. 91. Print.

"Ba and Ka: The Human Soul In Ancient Egypt." *Ancient Egyptian Articles*. KingTutOne.com, n.d. Web.

Basler, Roy P. "Selected Quotations by Abraham Lincoln." *Responsibility*. Abraham Lincoln Online, 2013. Web.

"Beta Israel." *Wikipedia*. Wikimedia Foundation, 9 May 2014. Web.

"Bilocation." *Catholic Encyclopedia*. Catholic Online, 2013. Web.

"Blade Runner (1982) Quotes." *IMDb*. Amazon, 2014. Web.

Bibliography

Blanke, Olaf. "Induction of an illusory shadow person." Abstract. *Nature* 443 (21 Sep. 2006): 287. Macmillan Publishers Limited. Web.

"Book of Enoch." *Wikipedia*. Wikimedia Foundation, 2013. Web.

"Book of the Dead Chapter 125A." *Digital Egypt for Universities*. University College London, 2003. Web.

Boylan, Peter W. "Aikido as Spiritual Practice in the United States." *Aikido Articles: Spiritual*. AikiWeb, Dec. 1999. Web.

Brandon, Brian. "Exposing Martial Arts." *Writing*. VMTC - International, 2011. Web.

"Bruce Lee Quotes." *USA DOJO*. Martial Arts Enterprises, Inc., 2013. Web.

"Buddhism: Death's Messengers." *Sacred Writings: With Introductions and Notes*. Ed. Charles William Eliot. Vol. 2: 701. New York: P.F. Collier & Son, 1910. Google Books (digitized 31 Jul. 2007). Public Domain. Web.

"Buddhist Chanting - Paritta." *Maithri.com*. Maithri Publications, 2010. Web.

Buratti, Robert James. "The Spiritual Dimensions of the Martial Arts." *New Dawn Magazine*. NGCI Pty Ltd., 15 Jan. 2014. Web.

Cadwalladr, Carole. "Are the robots about to rise? Google's new director of engineering thinks so..." *The Guardian*. Guardian News and Media Limited, 22 Feb. 2014. Web.

"Cambodia." *The World Factbook*. CIA, 11 Apr. 2014. Web.

Campbell, Bronwyn. "Egyptian antiquities from the Louvre: journey to the Afterlife." *Previous exhibitions 2007*. National Gallery of Australia, 2006. Web.

Chopra, Deepak, and Michael Shermer. "The Great Afterlife." *Skeptic*. The Skeptics Society, 2008. Web.

"Christianity by Country." *Wikipedia*. Wikimedia Foundation, 2013. Web.

Cline, Austin. "Ah Puch: Ah Puch, God of Death in Mayan Religion, Mythology." *Religion & Spirituality*. About.com, 2014. Web.

CNBC. "Chuck Norris vs. Bruce Lee (April 12 on CNBC)." Online video clip. *Youtube*. Youtube, LLC, 24 Mar. 2009. Web.

Coopersmith, Nechemia. "Animal Souls." *Ask the Rabbi*. Aish, 2014. Web.

"Courtly Art of the Ancient Maya: Maya Gods." *Exhibitions*. National Gallery of Art, Washington, D.C., 2014. Web.

"Credo of Islam." *Association for Islamic Spirituality*. Texas A&M University, n.d. Web.

Bibliography

Das, Subhamoy. "Contributor Bios." *Religion & Spirituality > Hinduism*. About.com, 2014. Web.

Davidson, Baruch S. "Who made up the way we sing the Torah?" *Chabad.org*. Chabad-Lubavitch Media Center, 2009. Web.

Dickens, Charles. "Oliver Twist." *Educational Technology Clearinghouse*. University of South Florida, 2014. Web.

"Do animals have souls like human beings?" *Quick Questions*. Catholic Answers, 2014. Web.

Dunn, Jimmy. "Egypt: The Major Egyptian Books of the Underworld." *Feature Stories*. Tour Egypt, 12 June 2011. Web.

Edelman, Marsha. "Cantillation: Chanting the Bible." *Synagogue & Religious Music*. MyJewishLearning.com, 2010. Web.

"Einstein." *Metromnia (Newsletter)*. National Physical Laboratory, Winter 2005: Issue 18, 2-3. Web.

Elwell, Frank. "Alexis de Tocqueville: Equality and Democracy." *Presentations*. Rogers State University, n.d. Web.

Emspak, Jesse. "Spooky Quantum Entanglement Gets Extra 'Twist.'" *LiveScience*. TechMedia Network, 6 Nov. 2012. Web.

Eveleth, Rose. "Robots: Is the uncanny valley real?" *Future*. BBC, 2 Sep. 2013. Web.

"Famous Pablo Picasso Quotes." *Pablo Picasso: Paintings, Quotes, and Biography*. PabloPicasso.org, 2014. Web.

Fitzpatrick, Laura. "Is There Such a Thing as Life After Death?" *Time*. Time Inc., 22 Jan. 2010. Web.

Fuller, Thomas. "Crisis in Myanmar Over Buddhist-Muslim Clash." *NYTimes - Asia Pacific*. The New York Times Company, 10 Jun. 2012. Web.

Gauvain, Michel. "Dazu Grottoes." *Buddhism in China Series*. The Woodenfish Project, 2014. Web.

"Geronimo." *First People of America and Canada*. Turtle Island, n.d. Web.

"Ghost Lab S01E08 'Shadowman.'" Online video clip. *Youtube*. Youtube, LLC, 11 Dec. 2012. Web.

Ginsberg, Johanna. "Chant expert seeks 'healing of the spirit'." *Greater MetroWest News*. The New Jersey Jewish News, 22 May 2013. Web.

"Global Christianity - A Report on the Size and Distribution of the World's Christian Population." *Pew Research: Religion & Public Life Project*. Pew Research Center, 19 Dec. 2011. Web.

Graziano, Michael. "Why is Music a Religious Experience?" *The Huffington Post*. AOL Family, 15 Jun. 2011. Web.

Bibliography

Gunther, Michael D. "Wheel of Reincarnation." *China - Baodingshan Rock Carvings*. Art-and-Archeology.com, n.d. Web.

Hafele, J.C., and Richard E. Keating. "Around-the-World Atomic Clocks: Predicted Relativistic Time Gains." *Science*. Science Magazine, 14 July 1972: 177 (4044) pg. 166-168. Web. Abstract.

Hardon, John A. "The Doctrine of Purgatory." *Father John A. Hardon, S.J. Archives*. Real Presence Eucharistic Education and Adoration Association, 2000. Web.

Hart, Hugh. "The Dark Side of Anime 'Innocence'." *SFGate*. Hearst Communications, Inc., 12 Sep. 2004. Web.

"Hinduism: The Book of the Separateness of the Divine and Undivine." *Sacred Writings: With Introductions and Notes*. Ed. Charles William Eliot. Vol. 2: 871. New York: P.F. Collier & Son, 1910. Google Books (digitized 31 Jul. 2007). Public Domain. Web.

Hitt, David. "What Is the Planet Mercury?" *In the Spotlight*. NASA, 30 Mar. 2011. Web.

Homer. *The Odyssey*. Ch. 11. Trans. Alexander Pope. London: Henry Lintot, 1752. Apple iBook. Public Domain. 04 Oct. 2010.

"Horizons of eternity: living and dying in ancient Egypt." *Events & Exhibitions: Video of Talks and Forums*. Queensland Museum, 2012. Web.

Hyams, Joe. *Zen in the Martial Arts*. New York: Jeremy P. Tarcher/Penguin, 1979. Print.

In Search Of. "1.19-Life After Death-In Search Of..." Online video clip. *YouTube*. Google Inc., 22 Aug. 2013. Web.

Ishiguro, Hiroshi. "Understanding the Mechanism of Sonzai-Kan." *ATR Intelligent Robotics and Communications Laboratories*. Osaka University, 2006. Web.

"Islam and Islamic History in Arabia and The Middle East." *Mosque & Religious Center*. IslamiCity.com, 2014. Web.

Kaku, Michio. "Robots." *Physics of the Impossible: A Scientific Exploration into the World of Phasers, Force Fields, Teleportation, and Time Travel*. Reprint Ed. New York: Anchor, 2009. 121. Print.

Karberg, Sascha. "Goethe's Doppelgänger." *Knight Science Journalism*. MIT, 1 Dec. 2009. Web.

Karuna, Kusala Ratna. "Do Buddhists go to heaven?" *Buddhist Afterlife*. t-dhamma.com, 2010. Web.

Katz, Ezra. "About Trope." *Lessons*. LearnTrope.com, 2009. Web.

Bibliography

Keane, Judy. "Why Gregorian Chant Rocks." *Catholic Exchange*. Sophia Institute Press, 15 Apr. 2013. Web.

Kirkland, Russell. "The Taoist Tradition: A Historical Outline." *Franklin College of Arts and Sciences*. The University of Georgia, Oct. 2002. Web.

Kohls, N., et al. "Spirituality: an overlooked predictor of placebo effects?" Abstract. *Philosophical Transactions of the Royal Society of London B: Biological Science* 366.1572 (Jun. 27 2011): 1838-48. PubMed. Web.

Kreeft, Peter. "Hell." *Featured Writing*. The Official Peter Kreeft Site, n.d. Web.

Law, Stephen. *Visual Reference Guides: Philosophy*. New York: Metro Books, 2007. 254-55. Print.

Lee, Jong Soo, and Linda Lee. Personal Interview. 19 Jan. 2015.

Lescarboura, Austin. "Edison's Views on Life and Death," *Scientific American* (October 30 1920), 123: 446, 458-460. Google Books. Public Domain. 27 Mar. 2012.

"Life in Ancient Egypt." *Online Exhibitions – Life in Ancient Egypt*. Carnegie Museum of Natural History, n.d. Web.

Lim, Han Nee. Email interview. 16 Nov. 2014.

Long, Jeffrey. "Foundation for the NDE website: A Labor of Love." *Dr. Jeff's Corner*. NDE Research Foundation, 1999. Web.

Lubow, Arthur. "Terra Cotta Soldiers on the March." *History*. Smithsonian Magazine, July 2009: 1-3. Web.

Luebke, David. "Canons and Decrees of the Council of Trent." *Department of History*. University of Oregon, n.d. Web.

Mahāthera, Suvanno, ed. Jinavamsa. "Kāma-Loka (The Sensuous World)." *The 31 Planes of Existence*. Penang: Inward Path, 2001. 32-33. Web.

Mahmood, Mustafa. "The Holy Qur'an And The 'Psyche'." *Psychology*. IslamicWritings.org, 14 Dec. 2003. Web.

Mark, Joshua J. "Egyptian Burial." *Ancient History Encyclopedia*. Ancient History Encyclopedia Limited, 19 Jan. 2013. Web.

Mark, Joshua J. "The Mayan Pantheon: The many gods of the Maya." *Ancient History Encyclopedia*. Ancient History Encyclopedia Limited, 19 Jan. 2013. Web.

"Mayan Gods & The Universe." *Yucatan Adventure*. Maya Foundation in Laakeech, Feb. 2012. Web.

"Maya Religion." *Encyclopedia of Death and Dying*. Advameg, Inc., 2014. Web.

Bibliography

McClenon, James. "Near-Death Folklore in Medieval China and Japan: A Comparative Analysis." *Asian Folklore Studies* (1991): Vol. 50, 319-342. *National Taiwan University*. Web.

Moore, Jeffrey. "Martial Arts and Religion." *Articles*. American Federation of Jujitsu, 2006. Web.

"Morihei Ueshiba Quotes." *Quotes*. BrainyQuote, 2014. Web.

Musser, George. "George and John's Excellent Adventures in Quantum Entanglement, Part Two [Video] | Critical Opalescence, Scientific American Blog Network." *Scientific American*. Nature America, Inc. 16 Mar. 2013. Web.

"Nerva-Antonine dynasty." *Wikipedia*. Wikimedia Foundation, Inc., 12 Aug. 2014. Web.

netholer. "Supernatural Science - Previous Lives." Online video clip. *YouTube*. YouTube, LLC, 10 Jul. 2011. Web.

Nocquet, André. 1995. "Aikido - Unification of body and spirit." *Life in Japan and Aikido practice*. Guillaume Erard, 2013. Web.

Norris, Chuck. "The Secret Power Within: Preface." *Penguin Random House Canada*, n.d. Web.

"NOVA ScienceNOW: Social Robots." *PBS Video*. Public Broadcasting Service, 2014. Web.

O'Brien, Barbara. "Chanting: A Basic Buddhist Practice." *Religion & Spirituality > Buddhism*. About.com, 2014. Web.

O'Brien, Barbara. "The Five Dhyani Buddhas: Amitabha Buddha." *Religion & Spirituality > Buddhism*. About.com, 2014. Web.

Occhiogrosso, Peter. "Native American Spirituality." *World Religions*. TheJoyofSects.com, 1 Oct. 2002. Web.

"O'Sensei Quotes." *Villa Rica Aikido Martial Arts*. Villa Rica Aikido, 2012. Web.

Pagngnananda, Jandure. "Buddhist Chanting." *Theravāda Buddhist Home*. BuddhistPage.com, 2014. Web.

Pinney, Christopher. *Photos of the Gods: The Printed Image and Political Struggle in India*. "Staging Hinduism." London: Reaktion Books, 2004. 27. ISSUU (2013). Web.

Pollard, Nigel. "Roman Religion Gallery." *History*. BBC, 17 Feb. 2011. Web.

Poorthuis, Marcel. Email interview. 12 June 2014.

"Putting the placebo effect to work." *Harvard Health Publications - Harvard Medical School*. Harvard University, 1 Apr. 2012. Web.

"Qin Shihuangdi." *Explore - Leaders and Rulers*. The British Museum, n.d. Web.

Bibliography

"Quran." *Oxford Islamic Studies Online*. Oxford University Press, 2014. Web.

Rajhans, Gyan. "The Power of Mantra Chanting: Why and How to Chant." *Religion & Spirituality > Hinduism*. About.com, 2014. Web.

Ramsland, Katherine. "Shadow People." *Psychology Today*. Sussex Publishers, LLC, 14 Jul. 2013. Web.

"Ray Bradbury Quotes." *BrainyQuote*. BookRags Media Network, 2014. Web.

"Religions." *The World Factbook - People and Society*. CIA, 2013. Web.

"Rev. Dr. Martin Luther King, Jr. Quotes." *MLK Day of Service*. Corporation for National & Community Service, 2014. Web.

Rich, Tracey R. "Life Cycle: Olam Ha-Ba: The Afterlife." *Judaism 101*. JewFAQ.org, 2011. Web.

Richert, Scott P. "Saint Anthony the Wonder-Worker." *Religion & Spirituality > Catholicism*. About.com, 13 Jun. 2013. Web.

Rinpoche, Tsem. "Baoding Shan Rock Carvings-Nic!" *Art, Architecture & Culture*. Tsem Rinpoche, 14 Apr. 2013. Web.

Robin, William. "His Music, Entwined With His Faith: At Heart of Arvo Pärt's Works, Eastern Orthodox Christianity." *The New York Times*. The New York Times Company, 16 May 2014. Web.

Rosenberg, Jennifer. "Franklin D. Roosevelt Quotes." *20th Century History*. About.com, 2013. Web.

Ruickbie, Leo. *A Brief Guide To The Supernatural*. Philadelphia: Running Press Book Publishers, 2011: 14, 17. Print. (Reprinted by Robinson, London 2012).

Rulu. "Introduction." *Buddha Sutras Mantras Sanskrit*. SutrasMantras.info, Mar. 2014. Web.

Sample, Ian. "Stephen Hawking: 'There is no heaven; it's a fairy story.'" *The Guardian*. Guardian News and Media Limited, 15 May 2011. Web.

"Sandro Botticelli." *Artists*. Artble, 2014. Web.

Schevicoven, Henk Jan van. "Ixtab." *Maya mythology*. Encyclopedia Mythica, 27 Dec. 1998. Web.

Schiffman, Richard. "How the Placebo Effect Proves That God Exists." *The Huffington Post*. AOL Inc., 31 Jan. 2012. Web.

Searle, Adrian. "Vicious circles." *The Guardian*. Guardian News and Media Limited, 12 Mar. 2001. Web.

Seddon, Keith H. "Epictetus." *Internet Encyclopedia of Philosophy*. The University of Tennessee at Martin, July 11 2005. Web.

Bibliography

"Sikhism: beliefs about life after death." *GCSE Bitesize*. BBC, 2014. Web.

Singh, Harpreet. Personal interview. 20 July 2012.

Sirry, Mai. "Weighing Of The Heart Ceremony." *experience AncientEgypt*. Experience-Ancient-Egypt.com, 2012. Web.

Slemen, Tom. "The Vardoger… a spooky encounter." *Wirral Globe*. Newsquest (A Gannet Company), 6 Oct. 2008. Web.

Smith, Daz. "What is Remote Viewing?" *Remote Viewing information & resources*. RemoteViewed.com, 2013. Web.

Strassman, Rick. Email interview. 21 Mar. 2015.

Strong, Eugenie Sellers. *Apotheosis and After Life: Three Lectures on Certain Phases of Art and Religion in the Roman Empire*. London: Constable, 1915. *Internet Archive*. Public Domain. Web.

Sullivan, Mary Ann. "Base of the column of Antoninus Pius, Vatican Museum." *Digital Imaging Project - Rome, Italy*. Bluffton University, 2001. Web.

"Svarga." *Wisdom Library*. WisdomLib.org, 17 Mar. 2014. Web.

Sweeney, Edwin R. "Geronimo Apache shaman: best known for his deadly raids in Mexico and the American Southwest, and for eluding the U.S. Army, Geronimo also claimed the power to heal." *Wild West* Feb. 2013: 29+. *General OneFile*. Web.

Tauber, Yanki. "What is a Soul?" *Chabad.org*. Chabad-Lubavitch Media Center, 2006. Web.

Terrill, Ross. "Serene Haven of Buddhist Art." *NYTimes - Archives*. The New York Times Company, 14 Jan. 1990. Web.

"Thailand." *2012 Report on International Religious Freedom*. U.S. Department of State, 20 May 2013. Web.

"The Afterlife in Ancient Egypt." *NOVA*. Ed. Susan K. Lewis. PBS, 3 Jan. 2006. Web.

"The Egyptian Afterlife." *Ancient Egypt: Science & Technology*. Boston Museum of Science, 2003. Web.

"The Life and Adventures of Buffalo Bill." *The West Film Project and WETA*. PBS, 2001. Web.

The Mahabharata. Book 17: Mahaprasthanika Parva: Section 3. Trans. Kisari Mohan Ganguli, 1883-1896. Internet Sacred Text Archive, 2006. Web.

"The Music of Islam." *Releases*. Celestial Harmonies, 1998. Web.

"The Music of Islam, Vol. 10: Qur'an Recitation, Istanbul, Turkey (CD)." *Tower Records*. Tower.com Inc., 2012. Web.

"The Quintessence of Chongqing Dazu Rock Carvings." *Arts - Sculpture and Carving*. Cultural China, 2014. Web.

Bibliography

"The Roman Empire: In The First Century - Religion." *Devillier Donegan Enterprises*. PBS, 2006. Web.

"The soul in ancient Egypt." *The Fitzwilliam Museum*. University of Cambridge, 2014. Web.

The Tibetan Book of the Dead, Or the After-Death Experiences on the Bardo Plane. Ed. W.Y. Evans-Wentz. Trans. Lāma Kazi Dawa-Samdup. Salt Lake City: Summum, 2010. eBook PDF.

"The Zhou Dynasty, Confucius, and China's Philosophic Traditions." *Asia For Educators - Weatherhead East Asian Institute*. Columbia University, 2009. Web.

"Through a Glass Darkly." *Harold B. Lee Library - Anthem for Doomed Youth: Writers and Literature of the Great War; 1914-1918*. Brigham Young University, 1998. Web.

Townsend, Tim. "Paranormal activity: Do Catholics believe in ghosts?" *Faith and Science*. U.S. Catholic, Oct. 2013. Web.

Tsukayama, Hayley. "Google releases tool to deal with your data after death." *Business - Technology*. Washington Post, 11 Apr. 2013. Web.

"Twenty-four Questions on Sacred Music." *Musica Sacra*. Church Music Association of America, 2006. Web.

Tyagananda, Swami. Personal interview. 28 May 2015.

Underwood, Steve. "Valley of the Kings - Pictures of spectacular tombs built for New Kingdom pharaohs." *Egypt*. Culture Focus, 2009. Web.

Vance, Erik. "Seeking to Illuminate the Mysterious Placebo Effect." *NY Times - Health*. The New York Times Company, 21 June 2010. Web.

"Vardøger." *WikiStrinda*. Strinda historielag, 25 Apr. 2012. Web, Google Translate.

Violatti, Cristian. "Confucianism." *Ancient History Encyclopedia*. Ancient History Encyclopedia Limited, 31 Aug. 2013. Web.

Walters, Barbara. "Heaven -- Where Is It? How Do We Get There?" *ABC News - International*. ABC News Internet Ventures, 20 Dec. 2005. Web.

"Weighing of the Heart." *Ramesses I: The Search For The Lost Pharaoh*. Michael C. Carlos Museum - Emory University, n.d. Web.

"What happens after death?" *FAQ > Sikh Beliefs*. RealSikhism.com, 2014. Web.

"What is Intangible Cultural Heritage?" *UNESCO Culture Sector*. UNESCO, 2012. Web.

Bibliography

Williams, Daniel. "At the Hour Of Our Death." *Time*. Time Inc., 31 Aug. 2007. Web.

"Woman experiences afterlife after giving birth." *WPBF 25 News*. WPBF-TV, 13 Nov. 2014. Web.

Wright, Craig. "Lecture 15 - Gregorian Chant and Music in the Sistine Chapel." *Open Yale Courses*. Yale University, 2014. Web.

Younus, Faheem. "Islam's Understanding of Hell." *The Huffington Post*. AOL Inc., 27 Aug. 2011. Web.

Yun, Hsing. *The Heavenly Realms and the Hell Worlds*. Trans. Amy Lam, & Colin Batch. Hacienda Heights, CA: Buddha's Light International Association, 2000. Print.

Zepps, Josh. "Sikhs in America: What You Need To Know About The World's Fifth-Largest Religion." *The Huffington Post*. AOL Inc., 6 Aug. 2012. Web.

Index

Abyss, the, 66–67, 117
  see also Hell
afterlife, vi–vii, 15, 17, 20, 43, 71, 99, 180–81, 195–96
  apotheosis and, 138
A.I. Artificial Intelligence, 223
Akashic records
  see records, Akashic
Al-Ghazali, 69
Al-Kindi, 68
Allah, 51, 66, 101–5, 119–20, 128, 156
  see also God
angels, 61–62, 64–67, 103–4, 107, 118, 121, 209, 235
  arch-, 64
  guardian, 65, 67
Animism, 55
apparitions
  see ghosts
Aquinas, Thomas, 69, 197
Aristotle, 96, 197
  see also philosophy, Greek
artificial intelligence
  see intelligence, artificial
Ash, Thomas, 69
astral body
  see body, astral
atheist, 6, 68–71, 127, 148, 227, 232, 235
Atwater, P.M.H., 33

Bible, the Holy
  angels in, 64–66
  animal spirits in, 56
  evil spirits in, 62–63
  ghosts in, 50–51
  Heaven in, 129
  Hell in, 118
  human spirit in, 8
Blade Runner, 221, 224–25
body, astral, 30
Botticelli, Sandro, 142–43
  see also religion: art and
brain, the
  consciousness and, 22, 29, 35, 82, 93, 153, 191, 212, 233
  death and, 6, 31, 191
  placebos and, 182
  psychedelics and, 93–96, 184–91
  visions and, 47, 53, 87
Buddha, 32, 79–84, 123, 131, 141, 157–58
Buddhism
  chant in, 157–59
  Mahayana, 32, 142, 157–58
  Pure Land in, 32, 158–59
  Theravāda, 157–58
  Tibetan, 29, 78–81, 191
  Zen, 94–95, 158, 171–73, 176–77
burial, 14, 17–21, 85

Index

chant, Native American, 150–52
chi, 162, 172–77
Chopra, Deepak, 200–1
Christ,
 see Jesus
Christianity
 Catholic, 44, 49, 56, 64, 105–10, 114–126, 142, 149–50, 163
 Eastern Orthodox, 59, 64, 105–9, 119, 148
 Gregorian chant in, 149–50
 Protestant, 49, 64, 105–11, 118–19, 124–26
Confucianism, 22–23, 139
Confucius, 22
Coopersmith, Nechemia, 57
cremation, 85, 91–92, 102

Dead Files, The, 41, 46
deities
 see gods,
demons, 59–64, 110–11, 144, 192–93, 236–37
devil, the
 see Satan
Dick, Philip K., 221
dimension, vii, 7, 32–33, 43–44, 83, 104, 123, 202, 209–12
 middle, the, 29, 39–40, 43, 47–51, 56, 59, 61–62, 67, 114, 120, 124, 210
 see also Purgatory
divine, vi, 9, 21, 51, 68–70, 89, 93, 107, 116, 128, 139, 148, 155, 163–64, 184, 195
djinn,
 see jinn
doppelgängers, 44–47

dualists, new, 233

Edison, Thomas, 180–1
Egyptians, ancient, 13–19
 Amduat and, 136
 ba and, 18
 Book of the Dead and, 16–19
 mummification and, 14–15, 18
Einstein, Albert, 196, 199, 208
electro-magnetic field (EMF), 42, 73
electronic voice phenomenon (EVP), 39, 63, 73–75, 120, 210, 233
Elijah, 51–52
Eliot, Charles William, 115
enlightenment, 79–82, 158, 176, 187
entities, 43–44, 53, 68, 83
Epictetus, 127
 see also philosophy,
evil, 8, 16, 21–23, 49, 60–63, 102, 108, 113–118, 153
exorcism, 63, 110
Exorcist, The, 104
extra-sensory-perception (ESP), 194, 202

funeral, 15, 31, 85, 92, 101, 139

Gautama, Siddhārtha
 see Buddha
Ghost Adventures, 40, 43, 64
Ghost in the Shell, 224
Ghost Lab, 53–54
ghosts, 123, 179–80, 210, 236

255

Index

hauntings and, 5, 47–48, 83–84, 91
hunting of, 40–43, 72
God, 34, 66–70, 86, 88, 90–91, 107, 129, 132
  see also monotheistic,
gods, 16, 20, 69–70, 136
  see also polytheistic,
grave, 102, 110
Guiley, Rosemary Ellen, 54

Hawking, Stephen, 31
Heaven, 66, 126–32
Hell, 82, 113–20
  punishments of, 103, 108, 140, 142–45
Hinduism, 84-89, 131,
  Bhagavad Gita of, 116
  Mahabharata of, 58–59, 87
  Vedic chant in, 152–54
Hyams, Joe, 170-3

immortality, 23, 197, 227
Inferno (Dante), 117–18
intelligence, artificial, 219–226
Ishiguro, Hiroshi, 220–21
  see also artificial intelligence
Islam, 100–5

Jahannam, 119–20
  see also Hell,
Jannah, 128
  see also Heaven,
Jesus, 51–52, 62–63, 106–8, 129
jinn, 51, 54, 104
Judaism, 92–100, 107–8, 129–30

cantillation in, 154–55
judgment, 15–18, 21, 101–3

Kaku, Michio, 203, 223
karma, 32–33, 82, 86, 91, 98
Keats, John, 9–10
ki
  see chi
Kreeft, Peter, 118–19
Kurzweil, Ray, 222, 226–27
  see also transhumanism

Lee, Bruce, 171–75
liberation, 89, 131, 142
  see also Hinduism; Buddhism
life, past, 212–16
  see also reincarnation
lifespan, 6, 60–1, 224, 226–27
Limbo, 117
Long, Jeffrey, 34–37, 195–96

Machiavelli, Niccolò, 137
Maimonides, 95, 98–99
martial arts
  spiritual and, 161–177
Mayans, ancient, 19–21
McClenon, James, 32–33
meditation, 169, 183–84
metaphysics, 190, 193
monotheistic, 84, 89, 92, 100, 105
Moore, Jeffrey, 174–75
morality, 57, 80, 98, 137*n*, 166, 188, 238
Muhammad, 101, 106, 155

Index

mummification
  see Egyptians, ancient: mummification and
Musolino, Julien, 232–35
mythology, 8–9, 45, 70, 91

near-death experience (NDE), 8, 27–37, 87, 190–91, 195–96
Nephilim, 60–62
neuroscience, 87, 148, 196
Neuroscience and the Soul, 196–98
Nimoy, Leonard, 34
nirvana, 82, 130–31, 141–42
  see also Buddhism,
Norris, Chuck, 175–77

Odyssey, The (Homer), 50, 62, 114
orb, energy, 52
out-of-body experience (OBE), 29–30, 190–191

paradise, 16–17, 21, 91, 128
paranormal, 41, 70, 75, 83, 179–80
Patton, George S., 213–14
philosophy, 22–23, 95, 153, 189–93
  Greek, 6, 9, 68, 127, 197
pineal, 176*n*, 184–85
planes, dimensional, 21, 88–89, 122–23
Plato, vi, 31, 96, 197, 213
  see also philosophy, Greek
Plotinus, 212–13
polytheistic, 20, 84, 88, 188
prayer, 85, 109, 157

psi, 192–94, 234
psychic, 202
Purgatory, 109–10, 122–26

quantum
  consciousness, 200
  entanglement, 199
  field, 201
Qur'an, the, 65, 101, 155
  chanting and, 156–57

Rajhans, Gyan, 152–53
records, Akashic, 237
reincarnation, 57, 82, 85–86, 96–100, 140–41
  accounts of, 213–16
religion
  art and, 16–18, 135–45
remote viewing, 202–4, 234
Republic, The (Plato), 31
resurrection, 102, 108, 110
Rinpoche, Tsem Tulku, 78–81, 142
Ruickbie, Leo, 41

salvation, 90, 108, 118–19, 125
Satan, 65–66, 109, 114, 118
Sellers, Eugenie, 138
shadow-people, 52–54
Shihuangdi, Qin, 22–24
Shintoism, 55
Sikhism, 57, 89–92, 132
silver cord, 30
  see also out-of-body experience (OBE)
sin, 66, 86, 97–99, 108, 123, 125*n*, 143

Index

soul, 14, 89, 232
  animal, 55-59
    see also Animism
  concept of, 8–10, 18–19, 70, 95, 101, 197
spirit, 150, 167, 196
  bilocation of, 44–45
  box, 42, 72–75, 210–11
  concept of, the, 8
  lost, 49–50
  possession of, 62, 104, 110–11
  worship of, 21–22
spiritual, 22, 81, 93, 153, 155, 184, 187
  development, 174
  growth, 161, 173
spirituality
  in music, 147–59
Strassman, Rick, 93–100, 183–94
  see also brain, the: psychedelics and
supernatural, 91, 102

Tanakh
  Torah and, 92, 96, 154
Taoism, 22, 139, 166, 173, 176*n*
time
  linear, 187, 208–9
  non-linear, 51, 209–10, 212
  space-, 204, 211, 238
  travel, 211
Transcendence, 225
transhumanism, 227
transmigrate,
  see reincarnation
tunnel, 27, 31, 34, 36, 209

Ueshiba, Morihei, 162–64
underworld, 20, 31–32, 114, 117, 143

vardøger
  see doppelgängers
von Goethe, Johann Wolfgang, 46–47

Watchers, the, 60

Younas, Faheem, 119–20

Zaffis, John, 201

www.ingramcontent.com/pod-product-compliance
Lightning Source LLC
LaVergne TN
LVHW052340080426
835508LV00045B/2890